Inner-city Missions

Greg Jackson

Copyright © 2024 Greg Jackson

All rights reserved.

ISBN: 979-8-218-43215-7

DEDICATION

First and foremost, I give all glory to my Lord and Savior, Jesus Christ.

I would like to take the time to thank everyone who has been a part of my journey and I thank you all for believing in me. There are many pastors and leaders who sewed into me, believed in me, and supported me from the beginning. I cannot name them all, but I would like to give special mention to Dr. William Glover, Pastor Gray Foshee, Pastor John Antonucci, Pastor Russ Hurst and Pastor Urban D. I also want to thank Paul and Ivette Lodato, Danny and Ginette Vera as well as Walt and Tasheekia Harris for their endless support and prayers.

A special thank you to my wife Carla Jackson, my mother-in-law Cindy Neville, my father-in-law Robert Thomas, and Lisa Hershman who God used to connect us.

A shout out to my homies Scott Free, John Huffman, Derek Issac, Steven Perez, Percy Perry, Vaniel Devallon and the BIC boys.

I dedicate this book in loving memory to my mother, Ethael Jackson, who was my first cheerleader.

INNERCITY MISSIONS

Copyright © 2024 Greg Jackson, all rights reserved.

No part of this publication may be published, stored in retrieval software, or transmitted in any way by any means – electronically, mechanical, photocopy, recording, or otherwise, - without the prior permissions of the copyright holder, except as provided by the USA copyright law

Scripture quotations *Scripture quotations from The Authorized (King James) Version. Rights in the Authorized Version in the United Kingdom are vested in the Crown. Reproduced by permission of the Crown's patentee, Cambridge University Press*

ISBN: 979-8-218-43215-7
Library of Congress Registration
Innercity Missions

Notification>Religion & Spirituality>Christianity>Teen Young Adult>
Leadership>Social Issues>Inspirational
Edited by Jennifer C. Tabora
Cover Design: Cone City Designs

Printing and Publication Authorship Program. Publication Filing and Production Two Girls and a Bible Papermill Printing Press www.twogirlsandabible.org

CONTENTS

	Dedication	iii
1	The Journey & the Call	1
2	Against the Odds	16
3	The Backyard Mission Field	35
4	Diversity	50
5	Stereotype	61
6	Mission DNA	68
7	Biblical Worldview	77
8	Bridge the Gap	90
9	Soul Harvest	102
10	Living Selflessly	110
11	America the Rich Mission Field	119
12	Supporting Intercity Missions	128
13	Community Through Communication	137

FORWARD

Hello, my name is Greg Jackson, and if you're holding this book, you are on the cusp of embarking on an extraordinary journey. Inner City Missions is not just a guide; it's a testament to the transformative power of reaching out, connecting, and making a difference in the urban cores that so desperately need our compassion and assistance. As you turn these pages, you will delve into the heart of inner-city missions, uncovering the challenges, triumphs, and undeniable spirit that drives this vital work forward. This book is your first step on a path that may challenge you, change you, and inspire you to be part of something greater than yourself. Welcome to your journey to the right way—the way of understanding, support, and relentless hope.

1 THE JOURNEY & THE CALL

In the heart of the bustling inner city, where concrete meets community, a different kind of journey unfolds—one that transcends borders without a passport. Inner city missions aren't a tale of distant lands; it's a narrative woven within the fabric of everyday streets, where the pulse of change beats to the rhythm of resilience.

Amidst the urban symphony of honking horns and distant sirens, individuals emerge as unsung heroes, navigating the intricacies of change on the very sidewalks they tread. This is a book of transformation rooted not in miles traveled but in connections made, where the geography of impact isn't measured in longitude and latitude but in the lives touched right where they stand.

As we embark on this journey, remember that your passport for inner city missions is not stamped with visas but with compassion—a currency exchanged in acts of kindness, understanding, and genuine concern for the well-being of those who call the inner-city home. Join us as we venture into the heart of change, where the destination is not a place on a map, but a transformative experience etched into the soul of the community. In the heart of Fort Myers, my mother, Ethel Jackson, stood as a beacon of strength in the face of adversity, tirelessly navigating the complexities of single parenthood. Three kids, one modest home, and a determination that echoed through the quiet corridors—we were a testament to her unwavering resolve.

In the Dunbar community, where the odds seemed stacked against dreams, my mother's commitment became a guiding light in the shadows. Growing up the aspirations I had woven into the fabric of sports—an avenue of escape and a pathway to purpose. However, the absence of a father figure left a void; a silence in the stands where cheers should have echoed, and a quiet corner in the locker room where advice should have been given. The journey to pursue my athletic dreams became a solitary walk. I navigated a maze of challenges without the compass of paternal guidance. Dunbar, with its whispered reputation, painted a stark backdrop against the canvas of my ambitions. The streets beckoned with their own version of purpose—a siren call that could easily lead one astray. Despite my mother's valiant efforts, the void left by the absence of a godly man in our home cast a long and dark shadow. Her determination was not a fortress, but the foundation. The attention of drug dealers and the magnetic pull of quick allure gave me a distorted sense of belonging.

The streets whispered promises of easy gains, an escape from the weight of unfulfilled dreams. In those alleys, the camaraderie among those who wielded influence within the neighborhood seemed to fill the void that ached within. It became a twisted dance, a symbiotic relationship born out of shared desperation and an unspoken understanding of life's struggles.

As I walked the tightrope between two worlds, my mother's prayers echoed in the background, but the allure of the streets drowned out their resonance. In the heart of the bustling inner city, my life took a perilous turn as the desire to fit in led me down a treacherous path. The allure of acceptance among peers came at a hefty cost, dragging me into a downward spiral of bad choices and regret. In the uncharted terrain of my life, akin to Paul's transformative journey on the road to Damascus, I embarked on a path that unfolded in ways I never could have anticipated. Little did I know that the twists and turns of this extraordinary odyssey would lead me to the place I am today. Facing a life sentence for robbery with a firearm, I stood at the precipice of despair, believing that hope had abandoned me. The shadows of my choices loomed large, and the weight of the consequences threatened to define the rest of my existence.

On the eve of my final court date, my public defender delivered a stark dichotomy of news that would reshape my destiny. "I have good news and bad news. Which would you like to hear first?" he asked, punctuating the solemnity of the moment. Opting for a glimmer of positivity, I requested the good news. In a heartbeat, the atmosphere shifted as he revealed, "The good news is they dropped your life sentence down." A surge of relief coursed through me, only to be tempered by the weight of the impending revelation. With a measured tone, he shared the bad news that echoed like a somber refrain. "But you're still going to prison for 5 years." The courtroom's gravity intensified as the realization settled in – a reprieve from a life sentence, yet a journey into confinement awaited.

On my way to the Orlando Reception Center, the beginning of my prison sentence loomed ahead like an ominous horizon. It was my first time ever going to the state penitentiary, and the uncertainty gripped me. Boarding the bus, the clinking of shackles added a surreal layer to the reality sinking in. As they shackled us with chains that felt uncomfortably tight, a surge of anxiety washed over me. What in the world did I get myself into? The bus, a vessel of transformation, carried not just bodies but the weight of lives altered by choices and consequences. As we arrived, the air thick with anticipation, the officers barked orders: "Everyone off the bus right now! Prepare to take all your clothes off. No talking." Once again, reality began to set in deep.

In the stark atmosphere of the Orlando Reception Center, the stripping away of personal belongings mirrored the vulnerability of our souls within. The journey continued as we were ushered to the prison barbers, where our heads were shaved clean, symbolizing a new chapter in our lives – bold and exposed. On our way to the dorms, the atmosphere thickened with tension as one inmate cast inappropriate glances at a female guard. The lead officer's stern command resonated, "Turn your head, inmate. You belong to the state now." This marked the beginning of a long journey, peeling back the layers to reveal the inside world of prison life. Walking through the prison dorm, the tension was palpable. Each cell housed two men, creating an uneasy intimacy in a confined space. As I stepped into my cell, a sense of anticipation mingled with the unfamiliar faces around me. My roommate, a surprising source of comfort in this harsh reality, extended a welcoming hand. Amid the concrete and steel, a subtle connection formed. "There's a church service tonight, are you going?" my roommate asked. In that moment, I felt a tug within – a call towards something greater. It was then that I realized God was guiding me on a path I couldn't resist, a path of redemption amidst the harsh echoes of a life left behind. Anticipation filled me as I eagerly awaited the evening service. There was an inexplicable desire to be in God's presence, surrounded by His people.

Stepping into the service, I sensed a profound connection, a tangible manifestation of God's presence. Those who had come from the outside brought with them a contagious energy, and their stories of triumph over adversity echoed through the prison walls. As they shared their journeys of redemption from behind bars, a flicker of hope ignited there within me. Their experiences became a beacon, illuminating a path I now longed to walk—a path towards the same transformative power they had found within the embrace of faith.

However, with the dawn of the next day, reality settled in. The thoughts of the arduous five-year journey that lay ahead echoed in my mind. The initial burst of hope faced the stark reality of the long road home, and the challenge of navigating the trials within the confines of the prison system. Despite the challenges, a sense of belonging began to form within me, particularly at the Orlando Reception Center. It felt like the place where I could navigate the remainder of my time. I submitted a request to stay in the area, only to face a harsh reality when I was denied. Orlando Reception Center was merely a temporary stop, not the permanent prison they deemed suitable for me. The following week marked a harsh transition as I found myself relocated to Lake Butler. As we disembarked from the bus, the officers came down hard on us, creating an atmosphere even more challenging than the initial location. The harsh realities of the prison system became palpable in this new, unforgiving environment. However, as the week unfolded, a subtle shift occurred. The officers, initially rigid and unyielding, began to treat us with a bit more humanity.

A turning point came when they granted all the inmates' access to the recreation yard. Amidst the open space, a remarkable scene unfolded. I observed a group of men engaged in worship, their collective faith creating a sanctuary within the prison walls. I walked towards them. As I approached, an indescribable sensation enveloped me – a tangible manifestation of God's presence came over me. As the yard recreation faded, the weight of an impending journey lingered, casting a shadow over the promise of a permanent camp on the horizon, scheduled for Monday. As the sun painted the sky with hues of warmth, our group gathered in the early morning, fueled by anticipation. A hearty breakfast in the chow hall fortified us for the day ahead. As we boarded the bus bound for our final camps, a tapestry of thoughts unfolded in my mind. An overwhelming anticipation gripped me—would the next camp introduce me to brothers in the Lord, forging connections that run deep? Longing for a fellowship with

Christian brothers, my heart echoed the silent prayer that the upcoming experience would be a convergence of shared faith and strength.

As Hamilton CI loomed ahead, a new chapter unfolded in my journey. Upon reaching Jasper, Florida, and stepping into Hamilton CI, a unique sense of comfort enveloped me. Despite the familiar routines of every camp. As time unfolded there was something distinct about this place. Stepping into the yard, I encountered a sight unseen in my last two stops—over 40 to 50 inmates engaging in fervent worship. Drawn to the gathering, I sat down to listen to one of the men of God preach the word. In that moment, a profound certainty settled within me; I knew this was the place where God intended for me to be. In the prison ministry, there were two influential brothers, Brother Dewey Armstrong, and Elder Pitts. They graciously took me under their wings, fostering my spiritual growth within the confines of the penitentiary.

One day, to my surprise, they asked me to preach a sermon. It seemed unbelievable, but they insisted, expressing their conviction that God was calling me to share the gospel. It was a pivotal moment, marking the beginning of a journey that unfolded within those prison walls. The moment I entered the circle of worshiping brothers at Hamilton CI, an instant bond formed, and the warmth of their love enveloped me. Their collective welcome was immediate, creating an atmosphere where acceptance and camaraderie became the cornerstone of our newfound connection. As the moment arrived for me to preach, an unprecedented sensation enveloped me—a profound presence of the Lord took hold of my entire being. It felt as if the very words I spoke were infused with divine power. A tangible force of God flowed through me, and to my amazement, all the brothers in the circle were moved to tears as the Spirit descended upon us, creating an indescribable moment of connection and shared spirituality.

In the aftermath of that powerful preaching moment, the call of God on my life became undeniably evident. It marked the beginning of a series of confirmations, solidifying the divine purpose unfolding within me. Behind the imposing walls of Hamilton Correctional Institution, life unfolded in a tapestry of untold stories and hidden talents. Miles Monroe's words echoed through my mind as I discovered a reservoir of potential within the confines of the penitentiary – a place where creativity and ability bloomed despite the challenges. Within the concrete confines, I encountered a diverse array of individuals, each possessing remarkable skills. It was a microcosm of society, where gifted songwriters, poets, doctors, lawyers, and more were confined, their potential stifled by circumstance. The penitentiary, akin to the graveyard, held the unrealized dreams of those whose talents were overshadowed by their circumstances.

As time passed, a sense of camaraderie emerged among us. I found myself in the company of brothers who, despite their predicament, shared a common bond of faith and creativity. Together, we explored the realm of Christian music, pouring our hearts and souls into lyrics that reflected our journeys and hopes. The prison talent shows and Black History Month events in the chapel became platforms for expression, displaying the depth of talent hidden within the incarcerated community. It was within these moments that the resilience of the human spirit became palpable, breaking through the barriers of incarceration to reveal the beauty within. By The chapel, a sanctuary amidst the stern environment, witnessed the transformation of our shared experiences into something truly extraordinary. As we stood together, singing, and sharing our stories, the harsh reality of prison life momentarily faded, replaced by the power of shared humanity and the boundless potential within even the most unexpected places.

In the heart of inner-city missions, behind penitentiary walls, a resilient community thrived, making the best of their circumstances. Amidst it all, Jesus stood at the center, and God's transformative presence moved above and beyond. Despite the challenges ahead, a sense of home away from home enveloped every moment. My journey began with hard labor in the yard at Hamilton Correctional Institution, cutting grass under the sun. Surprisingly, I found solace in those moments, dedicating time to deep prayer and communion with the Lord. As God saw fit, I was promoted to work in the chapel, a role I cherished deeply. Here, I had abundant opportunities to spend meaningful moments in His presence and delve into scripture. Building relationships within the chapel, especially with inmates, became a significant part of my mission. As they sought cards to send to loved ones, I became a source of support and connection, fostering a unique bond with those within the compound. In the gritty tapestry of inner-city life, I discovered profound truths within the confines of prison.

Life, a mosaic of choices, unfolded in the shadow of towering

INNERCITY MISSIONS

structures, where the key was crafting one's destiny. Every opportunity within those walls became a pivotal moment — a chance to set the compass towards a brighter tomorrow. At the heart of my transformative journey stood Hamilton Correctional Institution, a beacon of hope in the urban expanse. It outshone any other correctional camp, reminiscent of the early chapters of my odyssey. Amidst the hustle and struggle, the gates of Hamilton CI opened to a stream of churches, each carrying the transformative love of Christ. Their presence, like a constant tide of hope and inspiration, became the catalyst for redemption in the inner-city missions. As I reflect on the journey, I realize that in the heart of adversity, one can find a path to renewal, and in the embrace of that opportunity, a bright future awaits. As my two-year season at Hamilton Main Unit drew to a close, bidding farewell to the brothers I had forged meaningful relationships with left me with a mix of emotions. Despite the sadness, a profound sense of purpose guided me, compelling me to step beyond the familiar confines of the compound. In trusting God's guidance, I embarked on a new journey, acutely aware that these experiences were shaping me for a future I was yet to discover.

Awakening to a higher calling in the dimly lit confines of my prison cell, I awoke to the resounding voice of the Lord, setting the stage for a remarkable journey into the heart of inner-city missions. Little did I know that this divine directive would lead me to the doors of the Prison Work Camp, marking the beginning of an extraordinary chapter in my life. The call confirmed within moments of the divine proclamation, the prison officer's voice crackled through the intercom,

10

affirming the supernatural connection that had just unfolded. "Inmate Jackson, pack your bags," he declared, aligning with the sacred message I had received. It was a surreal convergence of the spiritual and the temporal, confirming that this mission was divinely orchestrated. Embracing the unknown as I hastily packed my belongings, a mixture of awe and anticipation filled the air.

Stepping into the unknown, I embraced the mission laid out before me, driven by a newfound sense of purpose that transcended the prison walls. The journey to the Prison Work Camp became a symbol of redemption and hope, I witnessed the miraculous growth of the field ministry within the prison compound. Blessed with the opportunity to shepherd this flock, I embraced the role of Pastor, leading my fellow inmates on a journey of spiritual discovery and redemption. The transition from inmate to pastor marked a profound transformation, both for me and the community within those prison walls. Preaching from the prison compound, I delivered a compelling message that resonated with the hearts of over forty men. Their hunger for spiritual nourishment surpassed the physical confines, creating an atmosphere of reverence and openness. The impact of the Word spread like wildfire, touching lives, and sowing the seeds of change. In the heart of the prison work camp, a profound connection formed with a brother named Elliott Daniels. Gifted and deeply devoted to the Lord, he became a pivotal figure in the unfolding of a divine plan. As our friendship deepened, a divine prompting stirred within me, compelling the realization that Elliott was meant to co-lead the prison field ministry.

INNERCITY MISSIONS

One transformative day, the spirit broke free, permeating the prison yard with its presence. In that sacred moment, we witnessed a revival that transcended the confines of the facility. Even those hardened by their circumstances were drawn to the spiritual awakening, as the power of God's love captivated their hearts. Amidst the confines of my prison sentence, the Lord's voice resonated, revealing a profound calling that extended beyond the prison walls. The clarity of His message grew more evident with each passing day, unveiling a purpose greater than my current circumstances.

As I reflected on the early years, dating back to 2002, the divine orchestration of events became apparent. God had been connecting the dots, laying the foundation for a journey that would transcend the limitations of the present. His foresight reached beyond the confines of time, allowing Him to see not only my past and present but to intricately discern the path He intended for my future. The revelation unfolded like a map, guiding me towards the realization that the call on my life was expansive and transformative.

During my prison sentence, I found myself standing at the intersection of purpose and destiny, ready to embrace the unfolding chapters of inner-city missions that awaited. In the intricate tapestry of our shared purpose, Elliott and I began crafting dreams within the confines of our prison sentences. The revelation of our calling unfolded before us like a map, igniting a desire to embark on a journey that was both expansive and transformative. As we huddled in the depths of incarceration, planning for our release, our dreams took shape. We envisioned a future where we could step beyond the prison walls, armed with a mission to bring about profound change in the lives of others. The vision was vivid, but the path was uncertain—we were dreamers without a clear roadmap. With anticipation and a shared commitment to making a difference, we stood at the intersection of our pasts and the possibilities of the future. The call to inner city missions beckoned, and though the exact details eluded us, the passion to impact lives burned brightly within our hearts.

Little did we know the unfolding chapters would reveal not just the challenges, but the remarkable beauty that lay ahead on this transformative journey. While God was intricately preparing me for the inner-city mission behind the Prison walls a surprising twist entered the story in the form of a new brother on the compound—Cheo Irvin, the son of NBA Hall of Famer Julius Irvin. At first, disbelief echoed through the prison walls as inmates shared rumors of his presence. Yet, to our astonishment, truth unfolded as Cheo found his place in the same dorm at Hamilton work camp, his bunk adjacent to mine. A unique camaraderie emerged as we navigated prison life together. In the confines of our shared space, Cheo, with a wealth of experiences tied to his father's fame, opened a window into a world beyond prison walls. He would proudly display pictures of his father with Hollywood actors, and we found solace in watching NBA basketball games, an unlikely connection formed right within the prison dormitory.

One day, as we delved into conversation, I asked Cheo about his life

INNERCITY MISSIONS

in the hills, surrounded by affluence and luxury. His response was a revelation, "Bro, to be honest, I never enjoyed the life of having everything. I went from the rich area to hang out with the project kids. I felt like everyone wanted me to be like my dad and fill his shoes, but I wanted something different." In the unfolding narrative of inner-city missions, this unexpected bond with Cheo Irvin became a poignant reminder that divine connections often materialize in the most unforeseen places, shaping our perspectives and influencing the transformative journey that lay ahead. In the depths of our conversations, Cheo's narrative emerged as a raw and poignant testimony to the complexities of life. His story became a mirror reflecting the universal truth that adversity knows no bounds, transcending social status and upbringing. As I listened, I realized that the lessons we exchanged were not just a dialogue between two individuals; they were whispers from the Lord guiding our paths.

As Cheo Irvin's time at Hamilton work camp prison neared its end, it felt as though the Lord had placed him there to offer me a brief insight into the complexities of having it all. This experience revealed that affluence doesn't exempt one from the challenges of living in a broken home. The backyard mission field extends beyond impoverished neighborhoods, reaching into the middle class and even the affluent, shedding light on the widespread impact of societal struggles. In the heart of societal struggles, the mission field extends far beyond impoverished neighborhoods, touching the lives of the middle class and even the affluent.

INNERCITY MISSIONS

As the morning sun pierced through the prison bars, a vivid vision unfolded. Lying in a bunk in the dorm, the journey began with a surreal walk through a hallway, leading to the gritty streets where homelessness, drug dealing, and prostitution coexisted. This was the moment when God unveiled a profound calling to me about the inner cities of America. The Lord, in His boundless grace, doesn't summon the qualified; instead, He qualifies the called. It's a divine paradox that transcends the limitations of human judgment.

In the midst of personal shortcomings and societal labels, the call was extended far beyond my condition. The vision was not about a pristine, faultless messenger but rather about a vessel transformed by grace. It wasn't a call for the perfect; it was a call for the willing, the humble, and the broken. It was a call that echoed through the chambers of a prison cell, reminding me that redemption is not reserved for the righteous but offered to the repentant. In that sacred moment, I realized that the mission field wasn't confined to a geographical location; it was a call to the heart, a call to extend compassion beyond the bounds of judgment. The Lord, in His infinite wisdom, had chosen the imperfect vessel, acknowledging that transformation often begins with those who understand the depth of their own need for it. As the vision carried me through the prison corridors and into the heart of societal struggles – homelessness, drug addiction, and prostitution – it became clear that this call was a bridge between the brokenness of my past and the transformative power of a purpose greater than myself.

The Lord's call is not restrained by the chains of our history; it is a key to unlocking a future saturated with hope and healing. This chapter serves as a testament to the universal truth that the call to the inner-city missions is not contingent upon our perceived qualifications. It is an invitation extended to the wounded, the imperfect, and the contrite. As we embark on this journey together, let us carry the assurance that our past may shape us, but it doesn't define our capacity to answer the call of God. The Lord's call is a whisper that pierces through the noise of our mistakes, inviting us to step into the transformative embrace of purpose and service. "Behold, the LORD's hand is not shortened, that it cannot save." Isaiah 59:1.

This chapter serves as a testament to the truth that the call to the inner-city missions is not contingent upon our perceived qualifications. It is an invitation extended to the wounded, the imperfect, and the contrite. As we embark on this journey together, let us carry the assurance that our past may shape us, but it doesn't define our capacity to answer the call of God. The Lord's call is a whisper that pierces through the noise of our mistakes, inviting us to step into the transformative embrace of purpose and yes, you, reading these words – God is calling you, not despite your circumstances but precisely amid them. This call echoes the transformative narrative woven into the fabric of humanity – a narrative exemplified by the apostle Paul, a man who once persecuted Christians and even stood witness to the burning of churches.

The story of Paul is a profound illustration that God's call transcends our past, our mistakes, and the shackles of our own doing.

INNERCITY MISSIONS

As he journeyed on the road to Damascus, little did he know that the very zeal that led him to persecute believers would be harnessed for a greater purpose. Paul was on the cusp of a transformation that would turn him from a persecutor to a missionary soldier on the front line of God's calling. The parallel between Paul's journey and our own lives is striking. It serves as a testament to the divine ability to redeem, reshape, and redirect even the most unlikely candidates into instruments of profound change. Paul's past did not disqualify him; instead, it became the raw material for a narrative of redemption, grace, and unyielding purpose.

As we contemplate the call to the inner-city missions, let the story of Paul be a source of inspiration and reassurance. Your past may carry scars, regrets, and moments of darkness, but it does not diminish the power of the call. It is an invitation extended to the broken, the flawed, and the seeking — a call that beckons you to embrace your unique journey as a steppingstone toward a mission greater than yourself. The inner city is not merely a physical location, but a symbolic representation of the hearts and lives entangled in the complexities of urban existence.

God's call is an unyielding force that seeks to unravel those complexities, offering hope, healing, and purpose in the very midst of the struggle. So, as we embark on this exploration of inner-city missions, remember that the call is not reserved for the perfect or the faultless. It is extended to you, right where you are, in the midst of your condition. Embrace the call, knowing that God specializes in transforming stories of brokenness into stories of redemption and grace. The journey ahead may be challenging, but it is also a testament to the undeniable truth that God is calling, and your response can be the beginning of a transformative adventure.

2 AGAINST THE ODDS

As I faced the daunting odds upon release from prison in 2005, the absence of a single dollar weighed heavily. Day labor became my immediate reality, epitomizing the raw struggle I was immersed in. It was during this tumultuous period that my mother emerged as a beacon of support, providing not just a place to stay, but unwavering strength that would prove crucial in shaping my journey toward inner city missions. At that point, the full picture eluded me, but little did I know gratitude for my mother's presence would become a cornerstone in the unfolding narrative of purpose and transformation. Reentering society after five years in prison presented a formidable challenge. The rapidly advancing landscape of technology accentuated my sense of displacement. Navigating this unfamiliar terrain, I grappled with a profound sense of loss and disorientation, yearning to find my foothold in a world that had evolved significantly. Driven by a profound goal to integrate into society, my search for a church led me to a nearby one on foot. Yet, a sense of disconnection prompted me to discontinue attending.

Despite the stirring in my spirit that God had more in store for me, moments of fear crept in. The call to the mission field was strong, but my lack of understanding about it and uncertainty about God leading the way made it seem impossible at times. Wrestling with these uncertainties became a part of the journey, testing my faith in the greater plan that lay ahead. Being on the mission field means grappling with odds stacked against you, especially when God has instilled a vision in your heart that might not be immediately evident to others. The path forward was unclear, and I grappled with the unknown, uncertain of how everything would unfold. Under the weight of the world's pressures, I reached a breaking point, reconnecting with old friends. Unfortunately, this led me down a destructive path for about two months, sliding back into selling drugs. The turning point came when we were caught making a delivery at a local bar, facing the stern decision of the owner to ban me from there or call the police where I would not receive a light sentence.

In a moment of reckoning, high on drugs in an apartment the following week, I felt the grip of an overdose and vividly saw images of hell. Pleading with the Lord for intervention, I implored Him not to allow me to succumb to such a fate. Miraculously, the next day marked a pivotal return to the right path, as I found myself back in a church, recommitted to the journey of redemption. Reflecting on the profound investment the Lord made in me within the prison walls, I recognized the immeasurable value of a life in Christ. Determined to embrace this new path despite hardships, I committed to holding on.

Meeting Derek Matthews, a fellow day laborer, led me to Mount Herman Ministries after an invitation. Attending with no church clothes, I sat inconspicuously at the back. Pastor Glover delivered a powerful message on "Christ versus Culture." During the altar call, hesitance rooted me in place, but a brother with a distinctive Jesus swag approached me. Overcoming my fear of non-acceptance, I joined him at the altar. The moment I reached it, the tangible power of God enveloped me. Pastor Glover, laying his hands on me, brought an overwhelming experience—I felt a divine connection, realizing this was the inception of a series of dots the Lord had been connecting behind the penitentiary walls. I began developing a clear understanding of what it truly means to press through, navigating challenges and uncertainties with unwavering determination. The was a new journey for me; I was accustomed to a life centered around the world, having spent most of my years outside the church.

Growing up in the projects of Dunbar, prison served as a training ground, but the real mission field unfolded outside those walls in the diverse terrain of America. Surrounded by the right people, accountability became a cornerstone of my journey. Percy Perry, a big brother figure, played a crucial role in keeping me grounded. He candidly addressed the importance of aligning priorities, emphasizing the need to get my driver's license and pull things together, all in recognition of the significant call of God on my life. His guidance and encouragement propelled me forward on the path toward greater things. The impactful messages from this brother resonated deeply, emphasizing that even when the odds are against you, prevailing is possible with God by your side. His assurance that God has your back and will make room for you. This spoke volumes and became a source of strength and conviction on my journey. Indeed, the Bible is rich with stories of hope against the odds, and the life of Abraham serves as a powerful example.

Despite feeling a calling to preach the gospel, uncertainty loomed as the outside world appeared entirely unfamiliar. The path resonated with me, a stark contrast to my initial post-prison visit. Pastor Glover's powerful and anointed teaching continues to inspire. Percy Perry, the man who urged me to the altar, revealed himself as a man of God and the head of the outreach ministry. Inviting me to join, he emphasized the importance of community and reassured me of God's calling on my life. His words echoed a promise that I would be all right surrounded by a community of supportive brothers. Joining the "Drawn Sword Street Reach" outreach ministry introduced me to a group of young brothers radiating a contagious passion for the Lord, each carrying a distinct Jesus swag. Witnessing their fervor during Friday night missions, especially the joy unspeakable moments as they prayed for and led people to Christ, left a profound impact. The sense of connection and family they fostered made me realize that once again, God was weaving together the threads of purpose in my life. The

INNERCITY MISSIONS

enthusiasm continued as we delved into impactful ministry classes at Mount Herman. Together with my fellow brothers, we prioritized discipleship, eagerly absorbing the teachings to fortify our understanding of the Word. Mount Hermon's reputation as the "Word Church" was evident in the diverse attendance on Wednesday nights.

Teen Challenge participants and college students from across southwest Florida gathered to hear Pastor Glover speak, creating a dynamic and immersive environment where the fire of God was undeniably moving. Serving as the pastor's armor-bearer became a significant role for me, offering a sense of fulfillment and connection to something special. Watching Pastor Glover's every move, observing his meticulous preparation, allowed me to glean valuable insights and contributed to a deeper understanding of service and dedication. Even though I found fulfillment in serving and ministry, a sense that the Lord was calling me to something greater persisted, echoing the revelations from my time in prison. The unfolding journey held uncertainties, especially as I faced daunting odds, working multiple jobs at the labor force while grappling with the challenges of not ever having a driver's license, which became a source of embarrassment for me. The path ahead remained uncertain, yet I held onto the belief that this was all part of a larger, purposeful journey.

Despite facing formidable challenges, he held onto hope, displaying confidence and unwavering faith in what the Lord had called him to do. Abraham's journey echoes the timeless theme that, with trust in God's calling, hope can endure even in the face of daunting odds. Against all hope, Abraham in hope believed and so became the father of many nations, just as it had been said to him, "So shall your offspring be." (Romans 4:18) The odds were against Jesus, even in the town of Nazareth, where skepticism prevailed. "Can anything good come out of Nazareth?" (John 1:46) reflects the prevailing doubts. Despite the odds, Jesus' life and teachings went on to reshape the course of history, illustrating that divine purpose can emerge from the most unlikely places.

My mother's declining health became a poignant backdrop to my mission. Each day, I carried the weight of uncertainty, fearing the impending departure that lingered like an unspoken truth. "What if she leaves us?" became a haunting refrain in my thoughts. In the quiet moments by her bedside, I found myself caught between two worlds – one of societal struggles and the other, a deeply personal battle. The mission to uplift the inner city collided with the intimate struggle to keep my mother in this world a little longer. I shared my fears with others, expressing the profound impact her departure would have on me. The vulnerability revealed itself not just in my words but in the very essence of my being, resonating with those who faced similar fears.

The year 2008 marked the painful departure of my guiding light, my mother Ethel Jackson. The impact of her absence hit me with a force I had never fathomed, leaving me grappling with the daunting question of how I could navigate life without her reassuring presence. The grief was a storm that threatened to engulf me, and in its turbulent waves, I found both the inspiration and the challenge to channel my pain into the mission that had become my life's calling. In the intersection of personal loss and community upliftment, I discovered a reservoir of empathy that connected me to the very struggles of those I sought to serve. The inner-city, much like the depths of my heartache, harbored stories of resilience, strength, and an unyielding spirit. It became evident that my mission was not just about physical transformation but a holistic renewal that echoed the emotional and spiritual regeneration I sought in my own journey of healing. As the pages of my life turned, the void left by my mother's departure began to shape the contours of my purpose. The raw authenticity of my grief became a catalyst for understanding the multifaceted challenges faced by those dwelling in the heart of the inner city. Each step in the mission was now fueled not just by a desire for societal change but by an intimate understanding of human experience and the profound impact of loss.

As life unfolded, an uphill battle with the odds stacked against me. Having never truly been on my own, my journey took an unexpected turn at the tender age of nineteen when I found myself behind prison bars. Before incarceration, I shared a home with my mother, and upon release, the prospect of navigating life without her was yet another daunting challenge I had to confront. Yet, amidst the turbulent currents of adversity, a subtle but profound lesson unfolded. It became evident that the Lord was orchestrating a unique curriculum, one that centered on teaching me the art of living entirely dependent on Him. The echoes of His guidance resonated in the stillness of my newfound independence, urging me to trust in His providence and surrender to His unwavering guidance. While I was rebuilding my life, I discovered that embracing the call required a profound shift—a relinquishing of my self-reliance and an embrace of divine dependence. The journey from incarceration to liberation was not just a physical transition; it was a spiritual metamorphosis. The challenges that seemed insurmountable became steppingstones, each revealing a deeper layer of resilience and an unyielding trust in the Lord's plan.

As I ventured forth, the call to serve the inner city took on a richer meaning. It wasn't just about uplifting a community; it was about sharing the transformative power of faith and demonstrating that, even in the face of adversity, one could find solace in divine guidance. The scars of my past became a testimony to the redemptive grace that awaited those willing to surrender and embrace the call to a higher purpose. In the relentless landscape of the mission field, challenges loom large, demanding an unwavering resolve. To tread this path, one must be not only fully persuaded in the calling the Lord has bestowed but also confident, even when confronted with skepticism and the whisperings of impossibility.

The mission's challenges are a crucible that tests the mettle of conviction, requiring a steadfast belief in the divine purpose. Amidst the doubting voices that echo with impossibility, the call to uplift the inner city demands an unshakeable confidence, rooted in the assurance that the Lord's plan transcends the limits of human understanding. The story of our mission is one forged in the crucibles of faith and unyielding determination. It began as a whisper, a gentle nudging in my heart that grew louder with each passing day. The message was clear: "Look to the Lord and follow His plan." It wasn't easy at first. The path was fraught with challenges, and doubt often crept in during the quiet, uncertain moments. But the scripture, Jeremiah 29:11, was my beacon, reminding me that the Lord had a purpose for me, plans to prosper and not to harm, to give a future filled with hope.

Our mission became a sanctuary, a place of refuge and hope for those who had been forgotten by the world but never by God. I've witnessed firsthand the transformative power of compassion and service. As I stand here today, I am in awe of how far we've come. What started as a small initiative has grown into a beacon of hope in the inner city. Looking back, I realize that this mission was never about providing services; it was about embodying the love of Christ, about being a living testament to His teachings. It's about creating a space where everyone is welcome, where stories of pain and loss are met with empathy and support, and where every act of kindness reflects God's love.

The journey wasn't easy, but it is profoundly rewarding. As I continue to "look to the Lord and follow His plan," I am filled with gratitude for the opportunity to serve, to make a difference in the lives of those around me. The Inner-City Mission is more than a project; it's a calling, a lifelong commitment to serve, uplift, and inspire. And if there are hearts to be touched, lives to be changed, and souls to be nurtured, our work will go on, propelled by faith and the unwavering belief in the power of love and service. Against the odds, keep pushing, no matter what. This guiding light through the darkest of times has been the cornerstone of my journey and the Inner-City Mission I've had the privilege to shepherd. The call for Inner City Missions is vital, an urgent whisper that becomes a roar among the neglected streets and forgotten faces of the city. "The harvest is plentiful, but the laborers are few." These words from Luke 10:2 resonate deeply with me, serving as both a reminder of the mission's importance and a rallying cry for those of us committed to this cause.

If you have picked up this book, it wasn't by accident. Is there a stirring within you? A gentle yet persistent nudge towards something greater than yourself. Or you seek understanding, a glimpse into a world where faith and action intersect, creating ripples of change in the most unexpected places. Whatever the reason, know that this journey we are about to embark on together is one of resilience, faith, and unwavering commitment to serving others, even, and especially, when the odds are stacked against us.

The path of inner-city missions is fraught with challenges. Every day, we are confronted with the harsh realities of poverty, addiction, and systemic neglect. Yet, in the face of adversity, there is a profound beauty in the resilience of the human spirit and the transformative power of community and faith. It is here, among the seemingly insurmountable odds, that miracles are born, and lives are radically changed.

This mission, this calling, requires more than simply good intentions. It demands a heart willing to be broken and then remade, eyes open to the harsh truths of hands ready to serve and uplift. It asks for perseverance—because there will be days when the weight of what we face seems unbearable, when resources dwindle, and when hope flickers faintly like a candle in the wind.

Yet, it is in these moments, when the road ahead seems impossible, that our faith is refined, and our resolve strengthened. "Keep pushing, no matter what. For every setback, there is a breakthrough, for every moment of despair, a surge of hope. And in every face, we serve, we see a reflection of the divine, a reminder of why we answered this call in the first place.

Our work in the inner cities is a testament to the power of love in action. It's a reminder that service is not just an act of charity but an act of faith—a belief in the potential for renewal and redemption in every person we encounter. In these pages, you will find stories of lives transformed, of sacrifices made, and of the incredible impact a group of committed individuals can have when they come together under a shared mission.

Remember, "The harvest is plentiful, but the laborers are few." There is a vast field waiting, ripe with the promise of change and the hope of a better tomorrow. This call to action is not just for the select few but for anyone who believes in the power of compassion and the imperative of service. If you've picked up this book, consider it a sign, an invitation to join a movement of individuals determined to make a difference, one life at a time.

Let this journey redefine what you thought was possible, and may it inspire you to action, no matter the odds. The call for Inner City Missions is vital—and it begins with you. Indeed, the annals of history are rich with tales of resilience, stories of those who persevered against all odds, leaving indelible marks on the fabric of our society. As we forge ahead with the mission of serving in the inner city, it's vital to remember and draw strength from these titans of perseverance and champions of change. Their journeys remind us that the path to significant impact is often laden with obstacles, yet surmountable with steadfast determination and profound belief in the cause.

President Abraham Lincoln, a figure of immense historical importance, stands as a towering example of resolve in the face of adversity. Guiding the United States through its most tumultuous period, the Civil War, Lincoln faced opposition not just from the opposing Confederacy but from within his own ranks as well. The weight of a nation divided, the loss of life, and the moral quandary of slavery could have overwhelmed any leader. Yet, Lincoln remained unwavering in his commitment to preserve the Union and end the moral scourge of slavery, enshrining his legacy as the Great Emancipator.

Dr. Martin Luther King Jr., another luminary of perseverance, led the charge against the formidable edifice of racial segregation and inequality in America. His leadership during the Civil Rights Movement, marked by nonviolent protest and eloquent oratory, sparked significant change amidst formidable opposition. King faced imprisonment, violence, and rampant racism, yet his dream of a society where individuals are judged not by the color of their skin but by the content of their character never wavered. His enduring legacy is a testament to the power of relentless advocacy for justice.

The list, indeed, goes on, encompassing countless others who have fought valiantly against the odds for causes larger than themselves. These historical figures, along with many unsung heroes, have laid the groundwork for the continuing struggle for justice, equality, and service to humanity.

As we engage in the vital work of inner-city missions, these exemplars of courage and tenacity serve as guiding lights. Their stories not only provide inspiration but also a blueprint for affecting meaningful change. Much like Lincoln and King, we are called to confront the challenges of our time with unwavering resolve and an unshakeable belief in the righteousness of our cause.

The road ahead may be fraught with trials, but the lessons of history are clear: with perseverance, faith, and collective effort, transformative change is within our reach. Let us, therefore, press on, buoyed by the legacy of those who came before us, committed to uplifting the most vulnerable among us and creating a more equitable and compassionate world. The harvest is indeed plentiful, and though the laborers may seem few, history shows us that even a small, dedicated group can change the course of history.

Your story is a poignant reflection of resilience, hope, and transformation that many will find inspiring. Growing up in Dunbar, Fort Myers, Florida, amidst such personal and social turmoil, and emerging with a desire to give back to your community is a testament to your strength and character. Here's a way you might structure your narrative, weaving in the themes of hardship, faith, and redemption:

In the heart of Dunbar, Fort Myers, Florida, where the shadows of struggle cling to the streets like morning fog, I embarked on a journey that few could have predicted. The dreams of my youth, filled with the echoes of cheering crowds and the glory of sports triumphs, were gradually drowned out by the harsh cacophony of street life. It was a descent that seemed inevitable, a path trodden by too many before me do. Yet, amidst the chaos, there was a flicker of something more, a whisper of a greater plan orchestrated by a higher power.

As a child, I remember the turbulent storms of my home life, where love and violence danced in a devastating embrace. Watching my mother endure such pain engraved deep scars within me, scars that seemed to dictate a future devoid of hope. Yet, it was in these moments of despair that I found an unlikely sanctuary in faith. Every morning, the 700 Club would cast a light into our dim living room, its messages of hope and prayer reaching into the depths of my young heart. I clung to those messages like a lifeline, dialing their number with the innocence of a child seeking solace from the tempest around me.

This connection to faith, as fragile as it seemed, planted the seeds of transformation within me. Despite the grip of the streets, the relentless

INNERCITY MISSIONS

pull of a life veered off course, there was a part of me that never stopped yearning for redemption, for a purpose beyond the immediate horizon of survival.

God, it seemed, had set me on a journey from the start—a journey that wound through the darkest alleys of Dunbar but promised a glimmer of light if only I dared to follow. It was a test of faith, a pilgrimage through the valley of shadows, with the afterlife always in my contemplation, a poignant reminder of the eternal stakes at play.

Years passed, each one a chapter in this unfolding saga of redemption. The streets, once my captor, became the very grounds upon which I sought to sow seeds of change. I realized that my story, marked by pain and struggle, was not meant to end in despair but to serve as a beacon to others. Giving back to my community became my mission, a way to transform the narrative of Dunbar from one of hardship to one of hope.

Today, I stand as a testament to the power of faith and resilience. The dreams of my youth may have been reshaped by the trials of life, but they were not diminished. In giving back to my community, I found a new dream, one forged in the crucible of my experiences. My journey, once a solitary walk through the shadows, has become a collective march towards light and redemption.

Looking back, I see now that every step, every misstep, was a part of a greater plan. From the prayers whispered to the 700 Club to the battles fought in the silence of my heart, it was all preparation for the role I was destined to play. In the brokenness of my home, in the turmoil of my youth, I was being shaped into an instrument of change, living proof that no one is beyond the reach of transformation. Before the dawn of time, in the silence before creation stirred, your life was already a masterpiece in the mind of the Creator. You are not an accident. You are not a mistake. Even before you took your first breath, even before you emerged into the light of the world from your mother's womb, God knew you. He saw you. And He proclaimed your life to be one of purpose, meaning, and incredible potential.

To you, the reader holding this book, feeling like you're adrift, untethered, and uncertain of your place in this vast tapestry of existence—know this: You've been destined for greatness. Yes, you. Reading these words, contemplating where your next step might lead. No matter the obstacles you've faced, the setbacks that have bruised your spirit, or the doubts that cloud your vision, your story is far from over. In fact, it's unfolding exactly as it was meant to.

The journey of your life, with its highs and lows, has been a path leading you toward fulfilling your destiny. Every challenge you've encountered, every moment of despair, has been a steppingstone, shaping you into the person you're meant to become. These experiences, as arduous as they may seem, are chapters in your incredible story, teaching resilience, fostering strength, and nurturing an unwavering spirit of perseverance.

INNERCITY MISSIONS

It's easy to feel insignificant in the vastness of the universe, to wonder if your hopes and dreams matter in the grand scheme of things. But remember, the same God who painted the skies, who set the stars in their places, and who orchestrates the symphony of creation, took the time to craft you in meticulous detail. You are His workmanship, endowed with unique gifts, talents, and a purpose that only you can fulfill.

Your presence in this world is not by chance but by design. Each day presents an opportunity to move closer to your destiny, to uncover the greatness woven into your very being. The challenges you face are merely opportunities to rise, to demonstrate the strength that lies within you, and to embrace the journey that is uniquely yours.

So, to you, the one reading this book, feeling a little lost or overlooked, hears this resounding truth: You are here for a reason. Your life is a testament to the power of hope, the strength of faith, and the boundless love of the Creator. Embrace your story with courage, for you are destined for greatness, and this is just the beginning.

Marrying Carla (Thomas) Jackson was a leap of faith, a testament to the kind of love that novels try to capture, and songs attempt to serenade. She, with her heart full of dreams and eyes sparkling with hope, stepped into our union with a bravery that left me in awe. Carla did what few dared—she left behind everything familiar, the streets that witnessed her childhood laughter, the skies under which she dreamt, and the community that had shaped her very identity. She did it all for us, for the promise of a future together, and for a love that whispered endless possibilities.

Moving to a new place, especially under the banner of marriage, is akin to planting a seed in untested soil. This was both our first marriage, and like two novices at sea, we had to navigate the turbulent waters of this newfound commitment without a map, relying solely on the compass of our love to guide us.

The odds, as they were, seemed like towering giants casting long shadows over our intentions. Friends and family, though well-meaning, often echoed the sentiments of caution. They spoke of the challenges of marriage, the adjustments and compromises it demanded, and the stark reality that love, alone, might not conquer all. But within these challenges, within this new life we dared to forge together, we discovered an undeniable truth—our love was not a fragile thread but a mighty tether, strong enough to pull us through the stormiest of seas.

Carla's sacrifice, her willingness to venture into the unknown for the sake of our union, became the cornerstone of our relationship. It was a love language all its own, speaking volumes of her commitment and belief in us. And as for me, witnessing her resilience, her strength in moments of uncertainty, I was inspired to be more, to be deserving of such a sacrifice, to ensure that the new world we were building together was one where she could find the same joy and fulfillment that she had left behind. The journey of marrying Carla Jackson, of embarking on a road less traveled, is a narrative still unfolding. It's a story of love's triumph over adversity, of finding home not in a place but in a person.

And as we continue to weave this tapestry of shared life, I am ever grateful, ever awed by the woman who saw in me, and in us, a future worth embracing, a future where, against all odds, we found love in its purest, most enduring form.

My first official job was at a place called Cornerstone Kitchen and Cabinets. It was a carpentry job. I had the opportunity to work with one of my brothers in Christ, who was not only a believer, but a very skilled carpenter I was hired known as his helper, we would literally get home to the wee hours of the morning having to get back up to do it all over again. In the weaving narrative of life, certain experiences stand out, molding us into the individuals we are meant to become. My journey into the realm of professional work began at a modest yet bustling establishment known as Cornerstone Kitchen and Cabinets. It wasn't just any job; it was my initiation into the world of carpentry, a craft that demands precision, patience, and a profound respect for the material.

The skills I learned under his guidance extended beyond the technical aspects of carpentry. He imparted wisdom on perseverance, the importance of a job well done, and the value of patience—lessons that have stayed with me, shaping my approach to both work and life. The experience was akin to an apprenticeship, not just in a trade but in how to live a life grounded in faith and purpose.

Reflecting on those days and nights spent in the workshop, I recognize how that period was a foundational chapter in my life's story.

It was there, amid wood shavings and the whir of saws, that I discovered much about my capabilities, my faith, and the profound satisfaction of creating with my hands. The journey from Cornerstone Kitchen and Cabinets would eventually lead me down new paths, but the lessons learned, and the bonds formed in that workshop have remained a cornerstone of my personal and development.

In the grand tapestry of our lives, certain threads stand out, vibrant and meaningful. My time at Cornerstone Kitchen and Cabinets, alongside a brother in Christ and expert carpenter, is one such thread—a rich and defining part of my journey. In the mission field, where souls are as vast and varied as a forest in the heart of spring, the laborers stand as sturdy trees amidst a grove, each one a testament to the resilience and strength granted by faith. The leaves, in their illustrious shades of greens and golds, are like the at hand. This job, however, was made even more significant by the presence of a fellow believer and master craftsman, a brother in Christ who would become my mentor and guide.

This brother, whom I had the privilege to work alongside, was not only a devout follower of Christ but also a remarkably skilled carpenter. His hands, weathered and wise from years of experience, moved with grace and assurance, transforming blocks of wood into pieces of art that were both functional and beautiful. I was brought into this world as his helper, a role that I embraced with both humility and eagerness. Together, we embarked on long days that stretched into the night, crafting and creating, our hands and hearts invested in every piece that emerged from the shop.

The work was intense, with deadlines looming and expectations always high. Every day presented new challenges, from intricate designs that tested our skills to the physical demands of working with stubborn materials. Yet, the satisfaction of seeing a project come to completion, of knowing that our combined efforts had created something of lasting value, made every drop of sweat worthwhile.

Our routine was rigorous. We would find ourselves leaving the workshop in the wee hours of the morning, bodies exhausted but spirits fulfilled, only to rise with the sun and do it all over again. This relentless cycle could have been overwhelming, but I found strength in the shared sense of purpose and the camaraderie that comes from working closely with someone who shares your beliefs and your passion.

This brother in Christ was more than just a coworker; he was a mentor in both carpentry and faith. As we measured, cut, and sanded, we would often engage in conversations about life, faith, and the ways in which our work could serve as a form of worship. He taught me that every nail driven, and every joint fitted was an opportunity to glorify God through excellence and dedication. His perspective transformed the way I viewed our labor, elevating it from mere work to a calling, a ministry of craftsmanship. Myriad challenges and triumphs each missionary faces. Some leaves are vibrant, pulsating with life, symbolizing the moments of unmistakable blessing and success. Yet, others are tinged with the sorrowful hues of autumn, representing the trials and tribulations that each servant of the Word inevitably encounters.

Just as leaves are essential for a tree's survival, converting sunlight into sustenance, so too are the obstacles on the mission field critical for personal growth and reliance on God. They are the photosynthesis of the spirit, where the harsh light of challenge is transformed into the nourishment of stronger faith and deeper connection with the Lord lol.

Consider the Apostle Paul, a missionary who, against all odds, spread the gospel across the ancient world. His journey, fraught with perils, shipwrecks, and snakebites, mirrors a leaf during a harsh storm, clinging to its branch. Yet, it's written, "I can do all this through him who gives me strength" (Philippians 4:13, NIV). This verse is the sunbeam breaking through the canopy, offering hope and renewal to the weary leaf.

Similarly, James 1:12 offers comfort and promise to those facing trials on their mission, saying, "Blessed is the one who perseveres under trial because, having stood the test, that person will receive the crown of life that the Lord has promised to those who love him." This scripture is like the rich, fertile soil from which the tree of faith draws strength, enabling it to stand tall and spread its leaves wide, no matter how fierce the storm.

As the seasons change in the life of a mission, so too do the leaves on the tree. Some are shed, falling gracefully to the ground, a poignant reminder of sacrifices made and the transient nature of our earthly endeavors. Yet, with each fallen leaf, the possibility for new growth emerges. It's a cycle of death and rebirth that echoes the very heart of the gospel—a call to die to oneself and to live in Christ.

In the grand forest of God's creation, every leaf tells a story, every branch a testament to endurance, and every tree a beacon of hope. The missionaries, against all odds, stand firm, their faith deeply rooted in the timeless truths of scripture. They are the living embodiment of 2 Corinthians 4:8-9, which declares, "We are hard pressed on every side, but not crushed; perplexed, but not in despair; persecuted, but not abandoned; struck down, but not destroyed."

Against all odds, in the mission field, as in the heart of a forest, there is an unbreakable spirit—a resilience that thrives on the Word of God, turning the challenges faced into the very air that breathes life into the mission.

3 THE BACKYARD MISSION FIELD

As Fort Myers weathered the storms of violence in 2012 and 2013, a deeper understanding of my role within this turbulence emerged. This understanding was significantly shaped by my faith and the powerful narratives found in scripture. The concept of the 'backyard mission field' began to resonate with me not just as a strategy for community engagement but as a divine calling, deeply rooted in biblical teachings.

Amid gunfire and loss, an echo from the Book of Jeremiah (29:7) whispered a divine truth, "Seek the peace and prosperity of the city to which I have carried you into exile. Pray to the LORD for it, because if it prospers, you too will prosper." These words, originally meant for the Israelites in Babylon, became a guiding light for me. Fort Myers, though not Babylon, was my home, my community, and my responsibility. If I sought its peace and prosperity through God's guidance, we all stood to benefit. The backyard mission field was not just a local endeavor but a living embodiment of Jeremiah's call to action.

Another scripture that influenced my journey was the Parable of the Good Samaritan (Luke 10:25-37). In this story, Jesus challenges us to redefine our understanding of 'neighbor' and demonstrates that acts of love and mercy are not confined to our immediate circle but extend to all, especially those in dire need. Our backyards, often battlegrounds of violence and despair, were also spaces where such acts of mercy could transform lives. The wounded lying on the road to Jericho were not unlike the youth in Fort Myers, caught in cycles of violence and in need of someone to extend a hand.

This parable taught me that the mission field is wherever there is a neighbor in need, often right outside our doors. It underscored the importance of getting involved in the gritty, everyday realities of those living in distress and offering hope and practical help. Our initiatives—whether they were after-school programs, community meals, or mentorships—became modern expressions of the Good Samaritan's compassion. In every act of kindness, we not only followed a biblical mandate but sowed seeds of peace and unity in our broken neighborhood.

The story of Jesus feeding the 5,000 (Matthew 14:13-21) further inspired our backyard mission. Faced with a vast crowd and limited resources, Jesus demonstrated that with faith, a little could be multiplied to meet the needs of many. This miracle encouraged us to start small, believing that our limited resources—when blessed by faith—could have a far-reaching impact. Each program we initiated, each life we touched, resonated with the miracle of the loaves and fishes, reminding us that scarcity is not a limitation when God orchestrates the outcome.

Drawn from these scriptures and others, the backyard mission field became a testament to the power of faith in action. It tied our personal journey of transformation to the biblical call to love and serve. As we navigated the challenges of intercity missions, these stories provided not just inspiration but a framework for understanding our efforts as part of a larger, divine narrative.

Our work in Fort Myers became a living scripture, a contemporary manifestation of God's love and power at work in the world. The backyard mission field—rooted in biblical teachings—became a space where faith was not just professed but practiced, where every act of kindness, every initiative, reflected God's love for a hurting world.

In embracing this scriptural foundation, the mission in Fort Myers transcended its initial response to violence and evolved into a profound journey of faith, hope, and healing. It reminded us that the work of restoration begins in the heart and extends to the farthest reaches of our communities, wherever there is a need, wherever there is a neighbor. In the heart of the bustling city, amidst the honks and the hurries, the mission was alive. Urban landscapes often painted pictures of modernization, yet beneath the towering skyscrapers and neon lights, there were souls yearning for a message of hope. It was here, in the cacophony of urban life, that the mission found its urgency. Inspired by a pivotal command, those called to serve remembered the words of Jesus, "But you will receive power when the Holy Spirit comes on you; and you will be my witnesses in Jerusalem, and in all Judea and Samaria, and to the ends of the earth" (Acts 1:8, NIV).

The command was crystal clear, yet profoundly deep, signifying a mission that begins at home—Jerusalem, then spirals outward to the ends of the earth. This framework laid out by Jesus wasn't just geographical; it was a blueprint for a strategic outreach, starting with one's immediate environment and gradually expanding to encompass the globe.

Jerusalem, the starting point, was symbolic for the believers. It was their home, their community, where their faith was most familiar yet faced immense challenges. The directive to begin in Jerusalem underscored the importance of witnessing to those closest to us—our families, friends, and neighbors. In the context of inner-city missions, the city is our Jerusalem. The streets we walk, the urban communities we are part of, are where our mission begins.

As the mission unfolded, the workers in the city discovered the profound beauty in starting their outreach at home. They found that the struggles and strife of city life often softened hearts, making them receptive to the gospel. The proximity allowed for consistent support and discipleship, fostering a community knit closely by faith. In drawing from the essence of Jesus' command, they realized that transforming a society begins with touching the lives of individuals in one's immediate surroundings.

The mission in the metropolis embraced the diversity and density of urban centers as fertile ground for the gospel. They saw in every face a potential disciple, in every corner a place for ministry. From the homeless seeking shelter in the shadows of affluence to the wealthy ensconced in high-rises, the mission reached out, embodying the love and compassion of Jesus. They understood that to "go into all the nations" required a deep-rooted foundation in their Jerusalem, from where the ripples of their efforts would extend outward.

Bridging the scripture with their experience, the mission workers were reminded of the early disciples who, filled with the Holy Spirit, began their ministry in Jerusalem. Their boldness and unwavering faith amidst persecution laid the groundwork for the gospel's expansion. Similarly, the inner-city mission tackled challenges head-on, armed with faith and the conviction that the power of the Holy Spirit would guide their every step. In every conversation, every act of kindness, and every prayer, they were witnesses to the transformative power of the gospel. The city, with all its complexities, was their mission field, ripe for harvest. They remembered the breadth of Jesus' command, knowing that their efforts in the city were just the beginning. For just as the disciples ventured beyond Jerusalem, they too were poised to take the message of hope to every corner of the earth.

Through their journey, the inner-city mission encapsulated the essence of Jesus' directive. They illustrated that the command to go forth starts with an inward journey, serving and loving those in our immediate sphere. From Jerusalem to the ends of the earth, the mission continues, propelled by the unwavering conviction that every soul encountered is a divine appointment, an opportunity to share the life-altering message of the gospel. That moment struck me deeply. The violence and despair that plagued the streets of Fort Myers, Florida, had long been a thorn in my side, a constant reminder of the brokenness that surrounded us. Yet, in the face of such turmoil, I had found myself trapped in a cycle of complaint and inaction. It was as if I had been asleep, blind to the power and responsibility that lay within my grasp. But the Lord's challenge awakened me: "Do something about it." Suddenly, the scriptures I had read so many times before took on a new life, their words not just a distant command but a personal call to action. James 2:14-17 echoed in my mind, "What good is it, my brothers and sisters, if someone claims to have faith but has no deeds? Can such faith save them? Suppose a brother or a sister is without clothes and daily food. If one of you says to them, 'Go in peace; keep warm and well fed,' but does nothing about their physical needs, what good is it? In the same way, faith by itself, if it is not accompanied by action, is dead."

Was I not doing the very thing James warned against? Claiming faith yet standing idly by as my brothers and sisters suffered in the streets? The violence, the hunger, the despair—they were not just issues to be debated or lamented. They were cries for help, opportunities for the church, for me, to put faith into action, to show the love of Christ in tangible ways. It was clear. I was being called not just to stew in the backyard of complacency but to cultivate a mission field right there, in the heart of the city.

With renewed purpose, I began to see Fort Myers not as a battlefield to be avoided but as a garden to be tended. The words of Jeremiah 29:7 resonated with me, "Also, seek the peace and prosperity of the city to which I have carried you into exile. Pray to the Lord for it, because if it prospers, you too will prosper." My mission was clear: to seek the peace and prosperity of Fort Myers, to be a beacon of hope and a bearer of Christ's love amidst the darkness.

The task was daunting, but I was not alone. The Lord had planted the same call in the hearts of many within our community. Together, we began to mobilize, to partner with local organizations, and to initiate projects aimed at addressing the root causes of violence and despair. We opened our church doors wider, offering not just spiritual solace but practical support—food pantries, job training programs, youth mentorship. We walked the streets, not in fear, but in faith, engaging with our neighbors, listening to their stories, and showing them, they were not forgotten.

In this journey, I learned a fundamental truth: the mission field is not a far-off place; it is right in our backyards. It is in the overlooked corners of our cities, in the eyes of the homeless man on the corner, in the tears of the single mother struggling to make ends meet. It is in the heart of Fort Myers, Florida, and in every city and town where God's children cry out for hope and healing.

By embracing this call to steward our backyard mission field, we became part of the solution. We saw walls of division begin to crumble, hearts transformed, and a community slowly knit together by the threads of God's love. And though the journey is far from over, we press on, fueled by faith and the unwavering belief that with God, all things are possible.

"Do something about it," He had said. And so, by His grace, we did. And in doing so, we discovered the beauty of being Christ's hands and feet in a world desperately in need of His healing touch. Continuing from that unforgettable evening, the success of the Taking the City Bash did not just mark the end of a victorious day but the beginning of countless intercity missions that would transform not just the local community in Southwest Florida but also set a precedent for future gatherings across various cities. The Backyard Missions, as they came to be known, was an initiative inspired by the scripture, specifically Isaiah 58:12: "Your people will rebuild the ancient ruins and will raise up the age-old foundations; you will be called Repairer of Broken Walls, Restorer of Streets with Dwellings."

The Backyard Missions sought to embody this verse by focusing on the most immediate spaces - the backyards of our homes and communities. It was a call to action for neighbors to come together, to rebuild not just the physical but the spiritual ruins that had long been neglected. It was about creating a sustainable impact that went beyond a single event.

After the overwhelming turnout at the Taking the City Bash, it was clear that there was a hunger for more. People were not just looking for music and entertainment; they were seeking a community and a deeper connection with God. This realization led to the establishment of monthly gatherings in different backyards across the city. Each meeting involved local artists, pastors, and volunteers coming together to provide not just spiritual nourishment but also addressing practical needs within the community such as food, clothing, and repair projects.

The BIC boys and Jericho, having witnessed the power of their influence at the bash, became regular performers and speakers at these gatherings. Their willingness to use their talents for God's work inspired many young people, drawing them closer to faith and service. The impact was profound, with testimonies of lives changed, families restored, and neighborhoods revitalized.

One remarkable story was that of a neighborhood known for its high crime rate, which hosted a Backyard Mission event. The local community, initially skeptical, gradually came forward, drawn by the music and the message of hope. That day, as the altar call was made, an unprecedented number of people gave their lives to Christ. In the weeks and months that followed, the crime rate in the area saw a significant decrease, and the community started a neighborhood watch program, turning their backyard mission into a continuous effort to care for and protect one another.

These Backyard Missions became a testament to the power of community and faith in action. They reminded everyone involved that the church is not confined to four walls but is found wherever people gather in God's name, be it in a grand auditorium or a neighbor's backyard. Each event, each gathering, sowed seeds of faith, hope, and love, fulfilling the scripture in ways that reached far beyond what anyone had initially imagined.

As the Backyard Missions continued to spread from city to city, they carried with them a message of unity, restoration, and divine purpose. They proved that when people come together under the banner of love and faith, there is no limit to the healing and transformation that can occur, both in the hearts of individuals and in the very fabric of communities. The narrative of the Backyard Missions became a beacon of light, displaying the incredible impact of collective action grounded in scripture and led by the Spirit, inspiring countless others to start their own missions in their backyards, wherever they may be. Nestled between the humble beginnings of a backyard and the sprawling outreach of a mission field lies a story that bridges the two worlds, transcending time, and geography. It's a narrative that finds its roots in the early 20th century with a figure whose impact on spirituality and community outreach resonates to this day—William Seymour and the Azusa Street Revival.

The backyard, in many cultures, is a space of growth, both literal and metaphorical. It's where seeds are planted, nurtured into life by the hands that tend them. It symbolizes a fertile ground for ideas, dreams, and spiritual awakening. Similarly, the mission field is a broader landscape, where these nurtured seeds are spread, taking root in diverse soils, flourishing into forests of faith that shelter countless souls. This dynamic interplay of growth and outreach can be metaphorically tied to the incredible journey of William Seymour and the revival he spearheaded on Azusa Street.

William Seymour, an African American preacher in the early 1900s, found himself in the backyard of society due to the color of his skin and his Pentecostal beliefs. Despite these barriers, or perhaps because of them, Seymour's faith and vision for a united church grew. He likened his own mission to that of a seed planted in the not-so-fertile grounds of racial and denominational divides. Yet, it was within a humble, makeshift building on Azusa Street in Los Angeles where this seed found its soil and began to sprout.

The Azusa Street Revival, beginning in 1906, was much like a backyard that welcomed all — regardless of race, gender, or social status — into a collective embrace. This revival, at its core, was a spiritual awakening that emphasized personal experience with the Holy Spirit, speaking in tongues, and miraculous healings. Under Seymour's leadership, this small space transformed into a mission field with limitless borders, breaking new ground in the way faith and worship were perceived. The revival meetings were the cultivation process, preparing individuals not just for personal transformation but for global spiritual outreach.

In this narrative, the backyard represents the microcosm of Azusa Street, an insignificant place where profound spiritual growth took place. The mission field symbolizes the Azusa Street Revival's ripple effect, spreading from a single point in Los Angeles to touch the hearts and souls of people worldwide. William Seymour, with his vision and faith, serves as the gardener, the missionary who saw beyond the backyard's confines and envisioned a field ripe for harvest, transcending cultures, and continents.

The legacy of Seymour and the Azusa Street Revival illustrates the power of faith and unity in overcoming societal barriers. It's a testament to how a single, humble origin can grow into a global movement, transforming backyards into mission fields. This narrative serves as a reminder that every significant movement begins with a simple step of faith, a seed planted in fertile soil, nurtured with hope and love. In the story of William Seymour and the Azusa Street Revival, we find the embodiment of spiritual growth and outreach, a beacon for those who aspire to bridge the gap between the intimacy of a backyard and the expansive reach of a mission field. Smith Wigglesworth, another monumental figure in the world of revivalism and missionary work, offers a compelling parallel to William Seymour's story, albeit with his unique backdrop and spiritual journey. Like Seymour, Wigglesworth's ministry found its roots in humble beginnings, yet his impact stretched across the vast mission field of the globe, demonstrating once again how a "backyard" faithfulness can burgeon into worldwide spiritual awakening.

Born into simplicity in 1859 in England, Wigglesworth's spiritual journey was as much a testament to personal transformation as it was to his eventual global influence. Initially a plumber by trade, Wigglesworth's life was radically changed when he encountered the Pentecostal movement, which ignited in him an unquenchable fire for God and His works. What makes Wigglesworth's story remarkable is how he, much like a diligent gardener in his own backyard, cultivated a deep, personal relationship with God before stepping out into the broader mission field.

Wigglesworth's ministry was marked by an unwavering belief in the power of faith and the working of miracles, which he carried like seeds from his own spiritual backyard into the wider world. His commitment to prayer, fasting, and studying the Scriptures was the fertile soil from which these seeds sprang. As he began to share his faith and witness to others, remarkable reports of healings, conversions, and revivals followed him, transcending cultural and denominational boundaries.

The parallel to the Azusa Street Revival and William Seymour's ministry lies in the transformative power of faith that both men exhibited, turning their respective "backyards" into thriving mission fields. Wigglesworth, much like Seymour, saw beyond the immediate horizons of their local communities to the potential harvest waiting in the world at large. Wigglesworth's ministry, characterized by his bold proclamation of the Gospel and his expectation for the miraculous, led him across continents, from Europe to North America, Australia, Africa, and Asia, planting the seeds of revival wherever he went.

What is particularly compelling about Smith Wigglesworth's story is how his "backyard" — the personal, intimate place of his own spiritual nurturing — never ceased to be central to his life, even as he stepped onto the global stage. His mission field expanded, but the essence of his ministry remained rooted in the simple, profound truths he cultivated in his early walk with God. He remained a man of one book, the Bible, from which he drew the strength and inspiration that powered his missionary journeys.

In drawing from the stories of William Seymour and Smith Wigglesworth, we see a vivid tapestry of how God can use individuals from humble beginnings to ignite fires of revival that warm the world. Both men faithfully tended their spiritual 'backyards,' cultivating a deep, unwavering relationship with God. And from these backyards, they stepped into vast mission fields, their lives serving as conduits for divine power and transformation. Their legacies remind us that the journey to global impact starts with faithfulness in the small, often overlooked places, proving that even the most unassuming backyard can be the birthplace of a movement that reaches the ends of the earth. During chaos, whether it be the historical tumult following the Rodney King verdict in Los Angeles or the persistent challenges facing cities like Chicago and communities across the nation today, the call for hope and transformation remains ever relevant and urgent. The turmoil and despair that cast long shadows across our society only underscores the vital role the church and individuals of faith must play in being bearers of light and hope. It's in these times of adversity that the Divine mandate to be effective in our own backyards gains profound significance, echoing the transformative ministries of figures like William Seymour, Smith Wigglesworth, and countless others who cultivated revival from the ground up.

The tumultuous days following the Rodney King incident in 1992, characterized by widespread riots, violence, and despair, brought the city of Los Angeles, and indeed much of the country, to a reckoning with issues of justice, race, and community cohesion. In such times, the message of hope can seem distant, almost unattainable, as the immediate reality of chaos and division takes precedence. Yet, it is precisely in these moments that the church is called upon to embody the very essence of hope, to minister to wounded communities and bridge divides with the message of reconciliation and peace.

The situation in Chicago, with its notorious reputation for crime and violence, similarly presents a daunting challenge but also an opportunity for the church to rise to its calling. The backdrop of crime and unrest, rather than deterring the mission, should instead galvanize it, serving as a reminder of the critical need for hope, healing, and transformation at the grassroots level. The church, in being present and active within such contexts, affirms the belief that no backyard is too desolate for hope to take root and flourish.

The enduring message for the church today remains one of unwavering hope and relentless pursuit of peace and justice, even, and especially, when faced with circumstances that defy such ideals. The history of revivals and transformative movements within Christianity demonstrates time and again that it is often in the midst of societal chaos and despair that the most powerful waves of spiritual renewal and community healing arise.

To minister hope for the world and for our own communities riddled with crime and strife, the church must first embody that hope. It means engaging with the very real issues that people face, not as distant observers but as active participants in the struggle for peace, justice, and reconciliation. This engagement starts in our own backyards, in the local communities where the impact of crime, poverty, and division is most acutely felt. It's about creating spaces where people can encounter hope in tangible ways, through acts of kindness, solidarity, and advocacy for change.

In essence, the call to be effective in our own backyards amidst chaos is a call to mirror the unyielding hope that has characterized the Christian faith throughout history. It's a call to remember that, even in the darkest moments, transformation is possible and that the church, equipped with the message of hope, has a pivotal role to play in ushering in that change. As we look to the examples set by those who have navigated similar challenges in the past, let us be inspired to act with courage and conviction in our own time, believing in the power of hope to renew our backyards, our communities, and our world. Jesus' ministry remains the quintessential blueprint for embodying real love and compassion, particularly in one's own "backyard." His approach to relationship-building, characterized by genuine interactions with those marginalized by society—tax collectors, sinners, and the disenfranchised—demonstrates a profound understanding of the transformative power of love and personal connection. Jesus didn't just preach from a distance; He engaged intimately with people's lives, breaking bread with them, sharing stories, and listening to their woes. This radical inclusivity and compassion challenged the societal norms of His time and illustrated His message of unconditional love and redemption.

Jesus' dining with tax collectors, exemplified in the story of Zacchaeus (Luke 19:1-10), was not just a simple act of sharing a meal; it was a deliberate statement about the nature of divine love and the kingdom of God. Tax collectors were viewed with disdain, seen as traitors and sinners for their role in collecting taxes for the Roman occupiers and often extorting their fellow Jews. By choosing to enter Zacchaeus' home and share a meal with him, Jesus showed that God's love knows no bounds and that transformation begins with acceptance and understanding, not judgment.

This approach to relationship-building, centered on love and compassion, illustrates the way Jesus controlled the atmosphere wherever He went. Instead of conforming to the prevailing attitudes of suspicion and exclusion, Jesus created spaces of welcome and healing. His presence invited openness, dialogue, and transformation. He demonstrated that true leadership and ministry are about meeting people where they are, offering them hope and a path to redemption.

For those looking to make a difference in their backyards amidst the contemporary chaos of our world, Jesus' ministry offers powerful lessons. First, it emphasizes the importance of being present and engaged within our communities, not as saviors but as fellow travelers sharing in the joys and struggles of life. It reminds us that relationship-building requires humility, patience, and the willingness to listen and learn from those we seek to help. Jesus' example teaches us that controlling the atmosphere—shifting it towards one of love, acceptance, and possibility—begins with our own attitudes and actions.

Moreover, Jesus' example underscores the role of the church not just as a place of worship but as a community of action, charged with bringing to life the principles of compassion, justice, and love in tangible ways. The church, following Jesus' lead, is called to be a sanctuary for all, especially those on the fringes of society. It's tasked with creating an atmosphere where transformation can occur, not through coercion or proselytization, but through genuine relationships grounded in love.

Jesus' way of engaging with tax collectors and sinners in His backyard is a clarion call for us today. It challenges us to look beyond societal labels and divisions, to see humanity in every individual, and to be agents of change through our own example of unconditional love and compassion. By doing so, we can control the atmosphere of our backyards, turning them into places of hope, healing, and new beginnings.

4 DIVERSITY

The inner cities of America, with their vibrant tapestry of cultures and communities, mirror the essence of the country itself - a melting pot of diversity where every person, regardless of their background, is a thread woven into the fabric of a nation. Missions within these urban landscapes are more than just outreach programs; they are living, breathing embodiments of scripture, translated into the multitude of languages and customs that make up the American ethos.

Matthew 28:19 commands, "Go therefore and make disciples of all nations, baptizing them in the name of the Father and of the Son and of the Holy Spirit." In the heart of America's urban sprawl, this directive takes on a profound significance. Missionaries are not required to cross oceans or traverse continents to find "all nations"; they need only to step into the inner cities to encounter the world in its entirety. Each neighborhood tells a different story, each face reflects a unique journey, and within these streets, the Great Commission unfolds not as a distant command, but as an immediate, vibrant reality.

The diversity within these missions is not merely a matter of varied ethnic backgrounds but encompasses a broad spectrum of socioeconomic statuses, languages, and experiences. It is in this diversity that the richness of the missions lies, for it is here that the unity of faith intersects with the multiplicity of cultures, creating a mosaic that is reflective of Revelation 7:9, which envisions a multitude from "every nation, tribe, people and language, standing before the throne and before the Lamb." The inner cities, in their complexity and vibrancy, are a foretaste of this heavenly vision, a place where the Kingdom of God is not a distant future but an emerging reality.

This diversity, however, comes with its challenges. Communicating the Gospel across cultural divides demands more than linguistic fluency; it requires an empathetic understanding of the nuanced differences that shape people's perceptions of faith, hope, and salvation. It calls for missions that are not only evangelistic but holistic, addressing not just spiritual needs but the physical and emotional scars left by poverty, inequality, and systemic injustice. Acts 17:26-27 reminds us that God created every nation from one man, intending for them to inhabit the whole earth, and that He marked out their appointed times in history and the boundaries of their lands. God did this so they would seek him, reach out for him, and find him, though he is near to all of us. Inner city missions, therefore, are positioned not just to preach, but to be the hands and feet of Jesus, serving and loving in a manner that reflects the creator's intention for unity amidst diversity.

The stories of transformation within these urban enclaves are a testament to America's identity as a melting pot — a place where differences are not just tolerated but celebrated as essential components of a larger narrative. Through service, prayer, and community engagement, inner city missions embody the essence of Galatians 3:28, where "there is neither Jew nor Greek, there is neither slave nor free, there is no male and female, for you are all one in Christ Jesus." In the bustling streets and quiet corners of America's cities, this scripture comes alive, offering a glimpse of a society where diversity is not a barrier to unity but the very means through which it is achieved.

In this chapter of America's story, inner city missions stand as vibrant reminders of the nation's foundational promise — a promise of liberty and justice, not just for some, but for all. Through the lens of scripture, these missions challenge and inspire, calling us to envision and work towards a community that fully embraces its diversity, recognizing in it the divine blueprint for a kingdom where every voice is heard, every culture honored, and every individual cherished. Pursuing the call to inner-city missions is an endeavor that demands not just a commitment to serve but a profound transformation of the heart—a transformation toward embodying the heart of God, particularly in crossing racial and cultural divides. This transformation is vividly illustrated in the encounter between Jesus and the Samaritan woman at the well (John 4:1-42), a narrative that serves as a foundational example of how we are called to engage with those whose lives are etched with the marks of societal divisions and prejudices.

In Jesus' time, Jews and Samaritans shared a long history of mutual enmity and disdain. Yet, Jesus intentionally crosses these deep-seated barriers to engage with a Samaritan woman, breaking not only ethnic boundaries but also challenging the gender norms of His day. This act of crossing borders was not merely a physical journey but represented a profound statement against the divisive prejudices of the time. Jesus' conversation with the woman at the well reveals God's heart posture toward humanity: one of unconditional love, acceptance, and a desire for true, life-giving connection beyond the constraints of societal divisions.

Furthermore, like Jesus' engagement with the Samaritan woman, pursuing inner-city missions with God's heart posture. To truly pursue the call to inner-city missions, one must cultivate this heart posture that Jesus exemplifies—a posture that views every individual not through the lens of racial, ethnic, or socioeconomic categories but as beloved creations of God, each with their own stories, struggles, and hopes. It requires a willingness to listen deeply, to engage respectfully, and to serve humbly, recognizing the image of God in everyone we encounter.

This heart posture is especially crucial in navigating the complexities and challenges of inner-city missions. The inner city is often a microcosm of the broader societal issues of racial and economic inequality, and missionaries are called to minister in contexts where the wounds of division and discrimination run deep. Embodying God's heart posture means actively working to bridge these divides, not through superficial gestures but through genuine relationships built on trust, respect, and mutual understanding.

And being willing to offer the living water of Christ—the message of hope, redemption, and transformation. It means seeing beyond immediate needs to the deeper spiritual thirst that only Christ can quench, and doing so in a way that respects and honors the unique cultural identities of those we serve. It is about being vessels of God's love and grace, facilitating encounters with Christ that can heal, restore, and unite.

To cross the racial divide in inner-city missions as Jesus did with the Samaritan woman requires a radical openness to God's transformative work in our own hearts. It demands humility, courage, and an unwavering commitment to see and celebrate the divine image in all people. As followers of Christ, we are called not just to serve but to love as He loved, to cross boundaries as He crossed them, and to embody the reconciling power of the Gospel in a world fractured by division and strife.

In embracing this call, we join in the larger story of God's redemptive work in the world, a story in which the walls that separate us are dismantled, and bridges of understanding and fellowship are built. The inner city, with all its diversity and challenges, becomes not just a mission field but a sacred space where the Kingdom of God is glimpsed in the breaking down of barriers and the coming together of hearts and lives transformed by the love of Christ. In the year 2019, as riots began to spring forth across diverse geographic locales, a palpable tension seized the air. These events were not isolated; they were symptomatic of deeper societal fractures, with narratives of racial division amplified through the media's relentless focus. In these tumultuous times, some within the body of Christ, overwhelmed by the chaos and swayed by the discord, stepped away from their posts, leaving a void where there was a profound need for understanding, unity, and guidance. This period of upheaval, however, was not merely a moment of despair but a pivotal opportunity for the church to step into its calling with renewed vigor and purpose. It beckoned the church to embody and demonstrate the ministry of reconciliation, rooted deeply in a biblical worldview and an understanding of how God sees His people.

The scripture articulates this divine mission of reconciliation in 2 Corinthians 5:18-19, where Paul writes, "All this is from God, who reconciled us to himself through Christ and gave us the ministry of reconciliation: that God was reconciling the world to himself in Christ, not counting people's sins against them. And he has committed to us the message of reconciliation." Through these verses, it is evident that reconciliation with God and among humanity is central to the Gospel message. The church's mission, therefore, especially amidst societal discord, is to be a conduit of God's reconciling love, bridging divides and healing wounds not with temporary band-aids but with the transformative power of the Gospel.

A biblical worldview reminds us that every person is created in the image of God (Imago Dei), as stated in Genesis 1:27. This profound truth transcends all human-imposed divisions including race, ethnicity, socioeconomic status, or political affiliation. Seeing people through this lens compels the believer to view every individual as a bearer of divine image, deserving of dignity, respect, and love. In the face of riots and societal unrest, this perspective shifts the narrative from one of division to one of shared humanity and potential unity under the banner of Christ's love.

The events of 2019 and similar seasons of upheaval expose the deep-rooted sin of racism and the brokenness it engenders within God's creation. They also highlight the urgency of the church's mission in the world—a mission that is not to conform to the divisive narratives prevalent in society but to offer a radically different narrative, one of hope, healing, and reconciliation through Christ. The church is called not to retreat in these moments but to lean in, fully embodying Romans 12:2's exhortation not to conform to the pattern of this world but to be transformed by the renewing of one's mind. Through this transformation, believers can discern and live out God's will—the good, pleasing, and perfect will that includes bridging divides and fostering healing.

In responding to societal chaos and racial divides, the church has a unique opportunity to demonstrate the ministry of reconciliation in tangible ways. This implies actively listening to those who are hurting, educating oneself and others on issues of racial injustice, creating safe spaces for dialogue and understanding, standing in solidarity with the oppressed, and advocating for systemic changes that reflect the Kingdom's values of justice, equity, and peace.

The ministry of reconciliation also involves a commitment to unity within the body of Christ, as emphasized in Ephesians 4:3, which urges believers to "make every effort to keep the unity of the Spirit through the bond of peace." This unity is not characterized by uniformity or the suppression of diverse perspectives but by a shared commitment to uphold the dignity of all people and to seek God's justice and peace in every context.

As the church embraces its mission to be ministers of reconciliation in a world marked by division and strife, it stands as a beacon of hope—a testament to the power of the Gospel to transform hearts, bridge divides, and usher in the shalom of God. Amid the chaos and confusion, this mission shines brightly, guiding the way toward a future where unity in Christ becomes a powerful witness to a world in desperate need of reconciliation. The Taking the City Bash has truly been a testament to the power of unity and diversity in the body of Christ, reflecting Jesus' mission to gather people from all walks of life toward a common goal—the soul harvest. This vibrant gathering has seen an incredible tapestry of individuals, each with their own stories, struggles, and triumphs, come together to celebrate, worship, and engage in meaningful community. This beautiful mosaic of humanity, united under the banner of Jesus' love, is a living embodiment of what it means to be the church in action.

Jesus' ministry on earth exemplified inclusivity and intentionality in reaching out to those who were often marginalized or overlooked by society. He dined with sinners, spoke to the Samaritan woman at the well, and healed the leper, amongst others, demonstrating God's heart for all people, irrespective of their background, social status, or past. In John 4:35, Jesus urges His disciples to "look at the fields! They are ripe for harvest." This statement is not just a call to evangelism; it is a declaration of the readiness and urgency for soul harvest—a harvest that encompasses every nation, tribe, and tongue.

The Taking the City Bash, in its essence, captures this vision of harvest. It is not just an event; it's a microcosm of the Kingdom of God, a glimpse of what happens when walls of division are torn down, and bridges of understanding and love are built. The diversity present at the bash is a powerful counter-narrative to a world often fragmented by differences. It is a declaration that in Christ, there is neither Jew nor Greek, slave nor free, male nor female, for we are all one (Galatians 3:28).

Drawing people from various backgrounds is not just about numbers or the optics of diversity. It's about enriching our collective worship and understanding of God. Each tradition, culture, and life experience bring a unique hue to our understanding of who God is and how He operates. The Psalmist declares, "Let everything that has breath praise the Lord" (Psalm 150:6). The diversity within the Taking the City Bash embodies this call, as every person, from every walk of life, brings their unique "breath" or spirit of praise to God, enriching the tapestry of worship and community.

Moreover, this gathering serves as a powerful witness to the world. In a society where division and isolation are rampant, the sight of a diverse group coming together in love and unity speaks volumes. It is a testament to the reconciling power of the Gospel and the beauty of the Kingdom of God, where every tear will be wiped away, and every division healed.

The task of soul harvest, as demonstrated at the bash, goes beyond the act of drawing people to an event. It involves sowing seeds of love, hope, and reconciliation, nurturing them with the truth of the Gospel, and reaping a harvest of souls transformed by the love of Jesus. This mission requires patience, persistence, and a deep reliance on the Holy Spirit to work in and through us.

As we reflect on the years of Taking the City Bash, let us be encouraged and inspired to continue this mission of bringing people together for the soul harvest. May we, as the body of Christ, continue to build bridges, celebrate diversity, and advance the Kingdom of God with one heart and one purpose. And in doing so, may we look forward to the day when every tribe, tongue, and nation will stand before the throne of God, united in worship and praise for eternity (Revelation 7:9-10). In the beginning, when the earth was without form and void, and darkness was upon the face of the deep, the Spirit of God hovered over the waters. With a voice as gentle as a whisper yet as mighty as a thunder, God spoke light into existence, separating day from night, crafting the expanse of heaven and earth, each with its unique purpose and beauty.

As the Creator moved over the waters, fashioning every creature that moves, every bird that flies, and every tree that bears fruit, there was a common thread woven into the fabric of creation - diversity. And it was good.

God, in His infinite wisdom, saw fit to mirror this diversity in His final and most intricate creation: mankind. "Let us make man in our image, after our likeness," He declared (Genesis 1:26). The breath of life was breathed into the first of humanity, and from one man, God made every nation of men, that they should inhabit the whole earth; and He determined the times set for them and the exact places where they should live (Acts 17:26). This divine tapestry of humanity was not a coincidence but a deliberate act of love from the Creator, celebrating variety in unity.

Over the ages, God's message to His creation has been clear and consistent. Through His word, He has reminded us that in His eyes, there is no Jew or Greek, there is neither slave nor free, there is no male and female, for you are all one in Christ Jesus (Galatians 3:28). This profound declaration is not a dismissal of our differences but an affirmation of our shared identity in the eyes of our Maker. It is a call to recognize the divine image imprinted in every soul, to cherish the rich tapestry of humanity that God Himself has woven.

As we navigate the narrative of diversity, it is crucial to reflect on the story of the Tower of Babel. Humanity's attempt to build a tower to the heavens was not condemned because of their unity in purpose but because of their pride and desire to make a name for themselves apart from God (Genesis 11:1-9). In scattering them and confounding their languages, God was not promoting division but rather illustrating the beauty of diversity within unity. This divine act was not to hinder communication but to enrich our collective journey, encouraging us to seek understanding, to learn from each other, and to grow together in love.

In the parable of the Good Samaritan, Jesus Christ Himself challenged the prejudices of His time, showing that our neighbor is not defined by race, nationality, or religion but by their need and our capacity to love (Luke 10:25-37). This timeless lesson serves as a reminder that the essence of our humanity lies not in our differences but in our shared ability to manifest love, compassion, and kindness.

As followers of Christ and stewards of God's creation, we are called to embrace diversity as a divine gift. We are urged to break down walls of division, to celebrate our differences, and to unite in our common humanity. For in Christ, we find the perfect example of love that transcends all boundaries, a love that sees no stranger but a brother, a sister, a reflection of God's image.

Therefore, let us strive to see the world and each other through God's perspective. Let us recognize that diversity is not just a concept to tolerate but a reality to celebrate. For in doing so, we honor the Creator who, in His infinite wisdom and love, made us all unique yet part of one human race, beautifully diverse and divinely united.

5 STEREOTYPE

In the days of Jesus, the tapestry of societal norms was heavily woven with stereotypes and prejudices. These biases were not only against groups of people but also against entire cities. Nazareth, the hometown of Jesus, was no stranger to such stereotypes. "Can anything good come from Nazareth?" was a rhetorical question loaded with skepticism and disdain. Yet, it was from this often-scorned city that Jesus embarked on His transformative intercity missions, challenging, and reshaping the prevailing judgments of His time.

Among the many encounters that exemplified Jesus' confrontation with societal stereotypes was the incident involving a woman caught in adultery. This event, unfolding in a bustling town square, served as a poignant tableau of the prejudgments and condemnations that were rampant in that era.

The air was thick with tension as a crowd gathered, their eyes filled with accusation and their hands ready to mete out punishment as prescribed by the law. The woman, accused and exposed, stood in the midst, a living embodiment of the shame and degradation society was eager to impose on her. It was in this charged atmosphere that Jesus entered, not as a spectator but as a challenger of the status quo.

His response to the accusers was neither a direct confrontation nor an acceptance of their judgement. Instead, He stooped down and wrote on the ground, as if to say that true judgment belongs not to man but to a higher authority. When He finally spoke, His words were a mirror to the conscience: "He who is without sin among you, let him throw a stone at her first."

One by one, the accusers left, confronted by the inconsistency of their own integrity. The woman, expecting condemnation, received from Jesus not endorsement of her action, but liberation from her immediate judgment and an encouragement to live a changed life. This incident was not merely about the woman caught in adultery; it was a vivid illustration of Jesus' mission to dismantle the stereotypes and judgments that held society in a vice-like grip.

INNERCITY MISSIONS

Jesus, the man from Nazareth, traversed cities, from the well-respected to the disdained, engaging with people who were often marginalized and stereotyped. Samaritans, tax collectors, lepers, and women like the one accused of adultery found in Him an advocate who looked beyond societal labels to their inherent worth as individuals.

His approach to intercity missions was revolutionary. Instead of upholding the stereotypes that divided people, Jesus sought to bridge gaps, build understanding, and cultivate a sense of shared humanity. Each encounter, each healing, and each teaching was a step towards dismantling the walls of prejudice.

The woman from the incident, forever changed, became a testament to the power of compassion over condemnation. Similarly, Jesus' acknowledgment of His roots in Nazareth served as a constant reminder that worth is not derived from one's origin, status, or the labels society might place upon them. Through His actions and teachings, Jesus illuminated a path of understanding, challenging His followers to see beyond the superficial divisions of their world.

In the wake of His intercity missions, Jesus left behind communities touched by an unexpected grace—a grace that called into question their deepest prejudices and invited them to view each other through a lens of empathy and kindness. This was the legacy of the man from Nazareth, whose life and work persist as a beacon of hope against the stereotypes that continue to divide humanity. In the rhythm of modern faith, where beats and prayers intertwine, the echoing sounds of

Christian hip-hop mark a profound evolution within church walls and beyond. It was not always this way; there was a time when the very notion of hip-hop in sacred halls was met with skepticism and resistance. Yet, through the perseverance of pioneers like Scott Free, Urban D (also known as Tommy Kyllonen), and Tre9 (Bobby Herring), a new chapter in worship and ministry unfolded, mirroring the transformative journeys of biblical figures who, too, faced opposition in their mission to spread a message of hope and change.

Scott Free, with his relentless determination, Urban D, with his vision for bridging urban culture and faith, and Tre9, with his commitment to outreach, became the architects of a movement. They laid the groundwork for a genre that would not only find its place within the church but also serve as a powerful tool for urban missions and youth outreach. Their journey was not without challenges; skepticism from traditionalists within the church mirrored the doubts faced by many biblical figures tasked with spreading a revolutionary message.

Much like Nehemiah, who faced opposition in rebuilding the walls of Jerusalem, these pioneers of Christian hip-hop encountered resistance in their mission to rebuild the perceptions of worship and ministry. Their work, however, was fueled by a conviction like that of Paul the Apostle, who traversed great distances and diverse cultures to spread the gospel. Paul, navigating the complexities of early Christian missions, resonates with the endeavors of these artists who sought to translate the timeless message of faith into a language that resonated with the youth and the urban communities.

The contributions of Scott Free, Urban D, and Tre9 extend beyond the realm of music; they represent a broader mission of inclusion and understanding within the Christian faith. Just as Jesus engaged with individuals from all walks of life, breaking down barriers and challenging societal norms, these pioneers of Christian hip-hop challenged the notion of what worship could look like, embracing diversity in expression and outreach.

Their legacy is one of innovation and courage, embodying the essence of urban missions. Through their art, they have opened doors for a new generation of artists and believers, allowing faith to be expressed in the multilingual, multifaceted tones of the modern world. The path they paved mirrors the journeys of biblical figures who, against the odds, laid the foundations for a faith that would transcend time, culture, and tradition.

In reflecting on the impact of these artists and the biblical figures who preceded them, it becomes evident that the mission of spreading hope and igniting change is as relevant today as it was millennia ago. The story of Christian hip-hop's acceptance within the church is a testament to the power of perseverance, vision, and faith in the face of adversity. It is a reminder that the message of love and redemption, regardless of the medium through which it is conveyed, remains universal.

As the beats of Christian hip-hop continue to resonate within church halls and city streets, the pioneering spirit of Scott Free, Urban D, and Tre9 lives on. Their legacy, much like the stories of biblical figures who paved the way for their faith, inspires a future where the arts and urban missions continue to evolve, united in their purpose to heal, uplift, and transform communities through the power of the gospel. For over two decades, my life has resonated with a rhythm unlike any other—a rhythm inspired by pioneers of Christian hip-hop and urban ministry. Like Scott Free, Urban D, and Tre9, who ignited a flame within the hearts of many, I too found my calling in the alleys and streets of the inner city. This journey, paved with beats, rhymes, and faith, has been both a mission and a test of conviction. Despite facing judgments and skepticism like those early pioneers, the directive from the Lord was clear: stay the course and continue to walk in love.

The essence of my mission has always been about bridging the gap between the church and those who view its towering steeples and echoing halls as alien landscapes—places where their stories, their struggles, and their truths might find no echo. These are the souls who wander the peripheries of society, often overlooked, yet they are the very people who Jesus Christ himself sought to reach. They need to know that the Lord can relate to every culture, every hardship, and every joy.

My endeavors in urban missions have not been without their challenges. Many from within the faith community have questioned the content and direction of our approach. They have argued that the beats and the bars may dilute the message, fearing that the sacred could become profaned by the secular. However, this journey has taught me that it is not about compromising the message but about making the message accessible. It is about speaking a language understood by hearts that beat to the rhythm of a different drum.

Embracing Christian hip-hop as a tool for urban missions was never about diminishing the gospel but about amplifying its reach. The streets have their own language, their own code, and to break through, one must be fluent in their narrative. It has always been about strategy—being relevant without relinquishing the core of our faith. It is a delicate dance of respect, understanding, and unconditional love.

There is a profound truth in recognizing that Jesus himself was the ultimate embodiment of cultural relevance. He spoke in parables, used the familiar to elucidate the divine, and reached out to those marginalized by society. Following in His footsteps, our mission is to be the bridge that connects disparate worlds, proving that faith is not confined to the pews but is alive in the streets.

As I reflect on the journey thus far, I am reminded of the countless lives touched by the willingness to venture into the unseen and the often misunderstood. There are stories of transformation, of hope rekindled, and of faith discovered in the most unlikely places. These stories fuel the flame of our mission, serving as beacons of what is possible when love transcends barriers.

Staying the course has meant enduring criticism and navigating doubts, both from within and from the outside. Yet, the call to walk in love remains unwavering. The urban mission field is ripe, teeming with souls yearning for a message that resonates with their experience, their pain, and their dreams.

The path of incorporating Christian hip-hop into urban missions is a testament to the adaptability and inclusivity of the gospel. It reaffirms that the Lord's love knows no bounds, reaching into every corner, every culture, and every heart. In staying the course, we echo the Lord's ceaseless pursuit of those who feel unreachable, proving that indeed, the church is not a building—it is a body, vibrant and alive, moving to the rhythm of grace in the heart of the city.

6 MISSION "DNA"

In the beginning, there was a code - not of zeros and ones, nor of chemicals and reactions, but of divine mission, yes, in Creation God has a Mission imprinted in the very essence of existence. This code, intricate and profound, was designed to guide, to inspire, and to transform. It was the DNA of purpose, a sacred sequence that pervaded all of creation, from the smallest grain of sand to the vast expanse of the cosmos. Within this divine blueprint was the story of missions, a narrative embedded in the fabric of reality itself, recounting the lives of those who walked the path of ultimate purpose.

Among these luminous threads were the Life of Jesus and Apostle Paul, figures not of flesh and blood within this story, but embodiments of missions that transcended time and space. Their essence, their teachings, and their lives were encoded within the cosmic DNA, serving as catalysts for change and beacons of hope.

Jesus, the embodiment of love and sacrifice, initiated a mission of redemption, his life a testament to the power of unconditional love. Through actions that spoke louder than the tumult of the world, he imparted a message that resonated through the ages, altering the very structure of the cosmic DNA. With every act of kindness, every word of forgiveness, and every gesture of compassion, he wove into the fabric of existence the codes of love, hope, and redemption.

Apostle Paul, once an instrument of persecution, became a conduit of grace. Transformed by a vision on the road to Damascus, his life took on a new purpose. "In him, we live and move and have our being," he declared, recognizing that the essence of life itself was intertwined with the divine. Paul's missions across the lands, his epistles to the faithful, became the strands through which the divine code was propagated, connecting communities, transcending boundaries, and nurturing the seeds of faith planted by Jesus.

Their lives resonate through the ages, influencing the course of history, shaping the contours of faith, and inspiring countless souls to embark on their own missions. The DNA of their divine missions intertwined with the fabric of human experience, prompting generations to seek deeper meaning, to strive for a higher purpose, and to live in a state of perpetual motion towards the realization of their encoded potential.

As this sacred code, this DNA of divine mission, unspools through time, it encounters resistance, doubt, and the ever-present shadow of despair. Yet, it perseveres, for within its helical structure lies the strength of those who have walked the path before, those like Jesus and Paul, whose lives serve as the template for all who seek to fulfill their inherent purpose.

And so, the story unfolds, not through the deeds of a singular character, but through the collective journey of humanity as it endeavors to decode the message woven into its very essence. It is a Life of discovery, of awakening to the realization that within each strand of DNA lies a mission, a divine purpose waiting to be fulfilled. Through the lives of those enshrined in the annals of faith, through their missions and their words, the path is illuminated, guiding humanity towards its ultimate destiny.

In this narrative of missions and DNA, where Jesus and Paul serve as the archetypes of divine purpose, the message is clear: within us all is the code of our mission, a sacred sequence inviting us to live, move, and have our being in a realm of divine potential, propelling us towards a destiny written in the stars, yet waiting to be discovered within the very core of our being.

In a bustling inner city, where the cacophony of urban life is ceaseless, there lived someone with an unquenchable desire to serve God fully. Amidst the hustle and bustle, everyday life seemed to overshadow the profound calling they felt deep within. It was a common narrative—a yearning to quit their 9 to 5 job to embark on a full-time mission, to serve God without distraction. But what they, along with many others, failed to recognize was that their life was already a ministry, a mission field ripe for sowing and harvesting.

Before the clarity of mission had dawned upon me, I, too, was ensnared by the notion that serving God required a grand exit from my day-to-day routine. I was convinced that the humdrum of my daily job was merely a holding pattern until I could break free and truly begin God's work. Yet, in those moments of inward reflection and through the gentle whispers of the Spirit, God showed me something profound—a revelation that shifted my entire perspective.

God had revealed that we carry His DNA, imbued with divine purpose, designed to embody His missions in action, right where we are. Our lives, regardless of our professions or daily routines, are full-time ministries. It was an epiphany that transformed the mundane into the sacred, infusing my every interaction, task, and moment with purpose.

Embracing this truth, I began to see my inner-city environment through a different lens. The people I passed daily on crowded sidewalks, the colleagues I interacted with, the neighbors living in the apartments next to mine—all were fields ripe for God's work. My mission field was not thousands of miles away; it was here, interwoven with the very fabric of my daily existence.

This realization ignited a passion to serve God in the now, not in some distant future after quitting my job. It led me to embody the essence of mission in my actions—sharing love, offering help, providing a listening ear, and being a beacon of God's grace to those around me. Serving God was not contingent on my job status; it was about being a living testament to His love and mercy every day.

The transformation was palpable. Colleagues began to inquire about the source of my newfound joy and peace. Neighbors felt comfortable sharing their burdens, knowing they had a compassionate listener. Even casual interactions with strangers turned into opportunities to demonstrate God's love in practical ways. My life, previously viewed through the lens of secular mundanity, was now a vibrant ministry alive with God's activities.

Understanding that our lives are full-time ministries revolutionizes our approach to everyday living. It compels us to recognize that every moment is an opportunity to serve God and embody His mission. We are equipped, through the Holy Spirit and the DNA of God within us, to impact the world around us profoundly.

Let this chapter serve as a reminder that we do not need to wait for "someday" or a "better time" to start living our mission. The mission field surrounds us, woven into the very essence of our daily lives. Our calling is here and now—to live out God's love and service in every interaction, to see the divine in the ordinary, and to understand that our lives are the most potent mission field.

At its core, realizing God's DNA in us propels us into a life of service. Just as Jesus came not to be served, but to serve (Matthew 20:28), we too are called to adopt this servant-hearted posture in all aspects of our lives. Serving others, then, becomes not just an activity we engage in but an expression of our very identity, whether we are at work, with family, or interacting with people.

So, as we continue our journey through the inner-city missions and beyond, let us carry this truth in our hearts. Our DNA is God's DNA, designed for purpose, action, and service, manifesting His kingdom on earth through our everyday lives.

Illustration: The Potter and the Clay

Imagine yourself as a lump of clay in the hands of the most skilled Potter. This Potter, God Himself, is shaping you, molding you into a vessel of His design. Each day, through the circumstances of your life, He presses and forms you, sometimes applying gentle pressure, other times firmer. You are being crafted not just for aesthetic purposes but for function. As a vessel, you are designed to carry the living water of God's love to those who are thirsty, to be a container of His grace and mercy. You are both the work of His hands and the instrument through which He pours out His blessings to others.

Metaphor: The Light

Consider yourself as a small candle in a vast, dark room. By itself, a candle's light might seem insignificant, barely illuminating the space around it. However, its true power lies not in illuminating itself but in its ability to pierce through the darkness. This candle represents your life, carrying the DNA of God, which is the Light of the World. Wherever you are placed, no matter how dark it may seem, you have the potential to bring light and warmth, to guide and comfort those lost in the shadows. Your small light can lead many to the source of all Light.

Scripture: Matthew 5:14-16 (NIV): "You are the light of the world. A town built on a hill cannot be hidden. Neither do people light a lamp and put it under a bowl. Instead, they put it on its stand, and it gives light to everyone in the house. In the same way, let your light shine before others, that they may see your good deeds and glorify your Father in heaven."

This passage beautifully encapsulates the essence of our mission DNA. It affirms that we are inherently designed to shine, to be visible beacons of God's love and grace. It is not about grand gestures or being on a distant mission field; it's about shining where we are, using our lives as platforms to illuminate the goodness of God. We are called to be living testimonies, our actions and words reflecting the Light we carry within us, drawing people to God not by our might but through the steady, gentle glow of His presence in our lives.

In summary, our mission DNA, as illustrated through the potter and the clay, as metaphorized by the light in the darkness, and as declared in

Scripture, positions us as active participants in God's kingdom work. We are crafted for a purpose, designed to carry, and spread His light, embodying His missions in the very fabric of our daily lives. Understanding God's DNA deeply intertwines us with His divine agenda. This understanding is not solely about acknowledging His existence or affirming His sovereignty; it is a call to a profound, transformative way of life. God's DNA within us beckons us towards a lifestyle characterized by commitment and devotion—a lifestyle where every choice, action, and thought are aligned with His will and purposes.

A Lifestyle of Service

We embody the hands and feet of Jesus, extending His compassion, love, and grace.

A Commitment to Love

Understanding God's DNA is also a commitment to love—unconditionally and sacrificially. 1 John 4:8 tells us that "God is love," suggesting that love is not merely an attribute of God but His very essence. To carry His DNA, therefore, means to commit to a lifestyle where love dictates our interactions, decisions, and relationships. This kind of love challenges societal norms; it forgives when wronged, gives without expectation in return, and embraces those whom the world often rejects.

A Devotion to Growth

This alignment with God's DNA also demands a devotion to

personal and spiritual growth. Just as a plant needs water, sunlight, and nutrients to grow, our spiritual lives require prayer, immersion in the Word, and fellowship with other believers. Devotion to growth means being intentional about nurturing our relationship with God, allowing the Holy Spirit to refine and shape us more into the likeness of Christ. It means being open to correction, eager to learn, and willing to step out in faith.

Living the Agenda

When we utterly understand and embrace God's DNA, His agenda becomes our agenda. His priorities shape our priorities. This divine agenda is centered on redemption and restoration—bringing people back into right relationship with God and mending the brokenness of creation. As carriers of God's DNA, we are invited to participate in this redemptive work, not as passive observers but as active co-laborers.

This lifestyle, commitment, and devotion are not borne out of obligation or an attempt to earn God's favor. Rather, they are the natural outflow of understanding who we are in Christ—created in God's image, redeemed by His sacrifice, and called according to His purpose. It compels us to live lives that reflect His character, to love deeply and serve faithfully, and to walk in a manner worthy of the calling we have received.

Understanding God's DNA is to embrace a life that mirrors His heart. It is a journey of transformation where we daily grow into the image of Christ, becoming vessels through which God's love, mercy, and grace flow freely to a world in desperate need. So, let us remember, we were created in His image, intricately fashioned to reflect His DNA, demonstrating His kingdom agenda to the world. This is not a mere theological concept meant for scholarly debate; it's a profound truth that has the power to transform how we live our everyday lives. Bearing God's DNA means we are mirrors designed to reflect His character, His love, and His righteousness in the corners of the world we inhabit.

Being made in His image provides us with a blueprint of our purpose here on earth. Just as a mirror has no light of its own but reflects the light it faces, we too are called to reflect the light of Christ, shining His radiant love into the dark places, bringing hope where there's despair, peace where there's turmoil, and love where there's hatred.

This reflection of God's DNA is not just about attending church services or engaging in religious activities; it's about embodying His kingdom's values in our day-to-day interactions. It is in the way we treat our neighbors, the integrity we show at our workplaces, the love and patience we extend to our families, and the kindness we show to strangers. Each action, no matter how small, is a potent demonstration of God's kingdom agenda to the world.

To reflect His DNA is to actively participate in His mission—to seek justice, love mercy, and walk humbly with our God (Micah 6:8). It is to use our God-given talents, resources, and time to serve others and advance His kingdom. It is understanding that our significance comes not from worldly accolades but from fulfilling the roles God has uniquely designed for us in His overarching plan.

Let us embrace this identity with both humility and boldness. Humility, knowing that it is by God's grace we are made in His image and part of His mission. Boldness, in confidently stepping out to demonstrate His love and righteousness in a world that desperately needs it.

As we go about our lives, may we continually seek to align ourselves more closely with God's image, allowing His Holy Spirit to mold us, refine us, and empower us. Let us be diligent in nurturing our relationship with Him, spending time in His Word, in prayer, and in community with other believers, for it's through these practices that we grow in understanding and reflecting His DNA.

In summary, remembering that we are created in His image to reflect His DNA is a call to action. It is an invitation to live out our divine purpose, showcasing His kingdom agenda through our lives. May we rise to this calling every day, demonstrating the love, grace, and truth of God to the world around us.

7 BIBLICAL WORLDVIEW

In the heart of the inner city, where the night seems to linger even during the day, a mission stands as a beacon of hope. The stories that unfold within its walls are not just tales of hardship and despair but also of redemption, transformation, and grace. The work carried out here is not merely a response to physical needs but a fulfillment of a biblical injunction to serve "the least of these" (Matthew 25:40).

The Foundation of Faith

The inner-city mission, with its myriad challenges, finds its foundation in a biblical worldview that sees every individual as created in the image of God (Genesis 1:27) and deserving of dignity, respect, and love. This perspective drives the mission's workers to serve tirelessly, often in the face of overwhelming odds. They understand that their service is not just an act of charity but an enactment of faith, a living testimony to the love of Christ for all, particularly the marginalized and the forgotten.

Meeting Needs: Beyond the Surface

The approach to service is holistic, recognizing that the issues facing inner-city residents are complex and intertwined. Poverty, addiction, violence, and hopelessness are but symptoms of deeper spiritual voids. Thus, the mission endeavors not only to meet physical needs through food, shelter, and healthcare but also to address spiritual and emotional wounds through counseling, education, and discipleship programs.

This dual approach echoes the biblical example of Jesus, who fed the hungry and healed the sick while also ministering to the spiritual needs of those He encountered. In the Gospel of Luke, Jesus proclaims, "The Spirit of the Lord is on me, because he has anointed me to proclaim good news to the poor. He has sent me to proclaim freedom for the prisoners and recovery of sight for the blind, to set the oppressed free" (Luke 4:18). The inner-city mission seeks to live out this mandate daily.

Building Bridges

In the modern context, the mission serves as a vital bridge between the church and the community. Often, the inner city is seen as a place of despair, overlooked, or avoided by many. Yet, the mission stands as a testament to the power of faith in action, drawing volunteers and resources from churches and individuals who are moved to support its work. In doing so, it not only brings aid to those in need but also awakens a sense of purpose and community in those who serve.

The mission's work also offers a powerful counter-narrative to the prevailing stories of division and isolation in contemporary society. By bringing together people from diverse backgrounds for a common purpose, it embodies the biblical vision of a united body of Christ, where "there is neither Jew nor Gentile, neither slave nor free, nor is there male and female, for you are all one in Christ Jesus" (Galatians 3:28).

A Living Epistle

As the mission goes about its daily work, it writes a living epistle of love, hope, and transformation. The stories of changed lives – of individuals moving from despair to hope, from addiction to freedom, from isolation to community – are a powerful testament to the gospel's relevance and power in today's world.

These stories also serve as a call to action for the church at large to engage more deeply with the world's pain and brokenness. In a society often characterized by indifference and cynicism, the mission's work is a reminder of the Christian call to be "salt and light" (Matthew 5:13-14), to bring flavor and brightness to the world.

The inner-city mission, grounded in a biblical worldview, stands as a beacon of hope during darkness. Its work, though challenging, is a vivid demonstration of faith in action, embodying the love and compassion of Christ for all. As it serves the physical, emotional, and spiritual needs of the inner-city community, it not only transforms individual lives but also offers a powerful witness to the relevance of the gospel in modern society.

In this endeavor, the mission invites all believers to participate, reminding us that the call to serve "the least of these" is not just a mandate for a few but a commission for the whole body of Christ to engage the world with love, hope, and the transformative power of the gospel.

The Lord's strategies are infinite, and His wisdom surpasses all understanding. It is through this lens that we should view our position in the modern world, especially when it comes to engaging with the spaces that seem overshadowed by spiritual darkness. Consider the public schools, bustling hubs of diverse thoughts, beliefs, and cultures. It is easy to perceive these environments as battlegrounds, places where the light of Christ might struggle to penetrate the prevailing shadows. However, it is crucial to remember that we are called not to shy away from darkness but to illuminate it. We are, as Scripture declares, "the city on a hill" (Matthew 5:14), tasked with the divine mission to radiate light in the darkest of places.

The Mission Field of Public Schools

Public schools present a unique and fertile mission field, teeming with young minds curious about the world and their place within it. If all Christian children were removed from these settings, we would forsake a critical opportunity to infiltrate the culture with the culture of Christ. Who, then, would be there to befriend the lonely, to speak words of kindness, to exemplify integrity, and to introduce the concept of unconditional love? Who would be the light?

The public school system, with all its challenges, is a place where young believers can learn to stand firm in their faith, to navigate the complexities of modern society through the lens of biblical truth, and to share the hope that is within them with gentleness and respect (1 Peter 3:15). This does not mean compromising on their beliefs but rather understanding and engaging with the world in a way that reflects the love and wisdom of Christ.

Equipping the Young

Equipping children and teenagers for this mission involves more than just imparting knowledge; it is about nurturing a deep, personal relationship with Jesus. It requires parents and church communities to invest in teaching them how to apply biblical principles to everyday situations, to discern right from wrong, and to seize opportunities to share the Gospel in word and deed.

Furthermore, it means encouraging them to see themselves as missionaries in their schools, equipped with the Holy Spirit's power to be agents of change. Just as Daniel was a shining example in the Babylonian court, and Joseph rose to prominence in Egypt without compromising their faith, young believers can stand out as beacons of hope and integrity in their schools.

A Collective Effort

The mission to illuminate the shadows is not solely the responsibility of the young; it is a collective effort that requires the support of the entire Christian community. Churches can play a significant role by providing prayer, mentorship, and resources. They can equip young believers with apologetics, helping them understand and articulate their faith, and create spaces where they can ask questions, voice doubts, and receive guidance.

The Promise of Presence

The encouragement to be the light in public schools and other spheres of modern society is undergirded by the promise of God's presence. Jesus assured His disciples, "And surely I am with you always, to the very end of the age" (Matthew 28:20). This promise holds true for young believers today as they navigate the challenges of being a Christian in a pluralistic society. They do not go alone into their mission fields; Christ goes before them and stands beside them.

The call to be a city on a hill is not a call to isolation but to vibrant engagement with the world in all its complexity and darkness. By encouraging Christian youth to remain within public schools and engage thoughtfully and lovingly with their peers, we foster an environment where the culture of Christ can infiltrate, transform, and illuminate the culture of the world. This is the essence of being the light—a visible, tangible presence of hope, truth, and love in places that desperately need it. To truly grasp the mission field of Western

America—or any mission field, for that matter—one must adopt a perspective that transcends the temporal and aligns with the eternal. It requires seeing beyond the immediate, understanding that the work of the Kingdom is not static but dynamic, evolving in response to the Spirit's leadership. The metaphor of changing seasons beautifully encapsulates this concept. Just as the natural world cycles through spring, summer, fall, and winter, so too does the mission field experience seasons of planting, growth, harvest, and renewal.

Understanding God's Perspective

The key to navigating these seasons lies in understanding God's perspective. This understanding comes from a deep engagement with Scripture, prayer, and a commitment to walking in step with the Holy Spirit. Isaiah 55:8-9 reminds us, "For my thoughts are not your thoughts, neither are your ways my ways, declares the Lord. As the heavens are higher than the earth, so are my ways higher than your ways and my thoughts than your thoughts." Adopting God's perspective means recognizing that His plans are often beyond our understanding and that our trust in Him must be unwavering, regardless of the season.

The Mission Field of Western America

The mission field of Western America is marked by its own unique challenges and opportunities. It is a landscape deeply influenced by secularism, materialism, and a pervasive sense of individualism. Yet, it is also a place of incredible potential for the Gospel to take root and flourish. To engage this field effectively, one must be prepared for the "seasons" it presents:

Spring (Planting): This season is about sowing seeds. In the context of Western America, this often involves building relationships, engaging in conversations about faith, and being a consistent presence in the community. It is about initiating projects that meet people's physical and spiritual needs, laying the groundwork for what is to come.

Summer (Growth): Growth is not always visible to the naked eye, but it is happening beneath the surface. This is a season of nurturing the seeds that have been planted—through discipleship, community engagement, and persistent prayer. It is a time when the groundwork laid in spring begins to bear fruit, though it may not yet be harvesting time.

Fall (Harvest): The harvest season is a time of reaping what has been sown and celebrating the fruit of the labor. In mission work, this can manifest as individuals coming to faith, the revitalization of communities, or the establishment of new churches. It is a season of visible change and transformation.

Winter (Renewal): Even in the mission field, there are seasons that seem dormant, where progress is hard to discern. Yet, winter is not a time of defeat but of preparation and renewal. It is a period for reflecting on the past seasons, seeking God's direction for the next, and resting in His faithfulness.

Moving with the Lord

A biblical worldview enables us to move with the Lord through these shifting seasons, trusting in His timing and His plans. It is about remaining faithful in winter as much as in the harvest, knowing that "in all things God works for the good of those who love him, who have been called according to his purpose" (Romans 8:28).

The mission field of Western America, with its ever-changing seasons, offers a unique opportunity to witness the manifold wisdom of God at work. Understanding these seasons from God's perspective enables us to engage effectively, adapting our strategies, bolstering our faith, and leaning into the work the Holy Spirit is doing in and through us. As we align ourselves with God's timing and purposes, we become instruments in His hands, ready to serve in whatever season we find ourselves. In the annals of history, few have demonstrated a commitment to a biblical worldview and the dissemination of Scripture as steadfastly as William Tyndale. His life's work, fraught with peril and pursued with unwavering conviction, was the translation of the Bible into English. His story is not just a historical account but a powerful testament to the transformative power of Scripture when made accessible to all.

The Vision

Tyndale's vision was revolutionary. In the early 16th century, the Bible was predominantly available only in Latin, a language accessible to the learned few. The common people of England, hungering for the Word of God, had no direct access to the Scriptures. Tyndale, deeply moved by this deprivation, committed himself to the translation of the Bible into English. His goal was clear: to make Scripture accessible to the "boy that driveth the plough" - in essence, to everyone, regardless of their station in life.

The Challenge

Accomplishing this mission was no small feat. The Church of England, under the sway of the Catholic Church, was vehemently opposed to any translation of the Scriptures into the vernacular. They believed that interpreting the Bible should remain the exclusive domain of the clergy. Tyndale's work was deemed heretical, a threat to the very fabric of the Church's power. He faced opposition, not just from the ecclesiastical hierarchy but also from the Crown. Yet, Tyndale's commitment to his biblical worldview - that every person should have direct access to the Word of God - remained unshaken.

The Work

Tyndale's work began in earnest, but it quickly became apparent that he could not complete this monumental task within England's borders. Facing mounting opposition, he left England under a pseudonym, continuing his work in Germany and the Low Countries. It was in Worms, Germany, that Tyndale's New Testament was first printed in 1526. This monumental achievement was not without risk; to smuggle these English Bibles into England, Tyndale relied on a network of supporters who shared his vision.

The Cost

The distribution of Tyndale's English Bible was met with widespread acclaim by the common people but with equal fury by the authorities. Copies were burned, and those found in possession of them faced severe punishment. Tyndale himself, betrayed by a friend, was captured near Brussels in 1535. After more than a year of imprisonment, he was tried for heresy, condemned, and executed by burning at the stake in 1536. His final words were a prayer: "Lord, open the King of England's eyes."

The Legacy

Tyndale's impact cannot be overstated. His translation laid the foundation for subsequent English translations of the Bible, notably the King James Version of 1611. His commitment to a biblical worldview, demonstrated through his life's work and ultimate sacrifice, sparked a transformation in religious practice, making Scripture accessible to the English-speaking layperson and empowering individuals to engage with their faith on a personal level.

Tyndale's unwavering dedication serves as a potent reminder of the power of Scripture and the importance of ensuring its accessibility to all. His story is a testament to the belief that the Word of God is a living, transformative force, meant to be shared broadly and freely, unhindered by language or decree. In the spirit of Tyndale, the mission field today continues to be one of translating, disseminating, and living out the Scriptures, grounded in the unshakeable truth of a biblical worldview. In the heart of Victorian England, a time characterized by industrial progress and spiritual questioning, there lived a man whose profound faith and eloquence made him a beacon of hope and guidance for many. This man was Charles Haddon Spurgeon, born on June 19, 1834, in Kelvedon, Essex. His story is not just one of religious significance but also of a transformative journey that impacted the lives of countless individuals across the world.

Charles was born into a Christian family, with his father and grandfather being preachers. Despite this, his journey to faith was neither straightforward nor devoid of struggle. As a boy, he was academically astute, with a particular fondness for reading. However, spiritual peace eluded him until one fateful day that would forever alter the course of his life and reaffirm his beliefs in the foundational truths of the Christian worldview.

It was a snowy day in January 1850, when Charles, then only 15 years old, was on his way to a scheduled appointment. The snowstorm grew so severe that he found his path obstructed, compelling him to seek refuge and solace. Guided by what he would later describe as divine intervention, he found himself entering a small Methodist chapel in Artillery Street, Colchester. The chapel was modest, with a congregation of merely a handful, and the absence of the minister that day meant that a layman, a shoemaker by profession, took to the pulpit to deliver the sermon.

The scripture for the sermon was Isaiah 45:22, "Look unto me, and be ye saved, all the ends of the earth: for I am God, and there is none else." The words, simple yet profound, struck a chord deep within

Spurgeon. It was as if the message was intended solely for him, addressing his internal struggles and doubts directly. The lay preacher's call to look to Christ for salvation resonated with young Charles, igniting a spark that would light the way for his spiritual journey.

This moment was pivotal, marking Charles Spurgeon's conversion and the beginning of his remarkable path as a Christian. He described the experience as seeing the gates of heaven opened and himself being ushered in—a vivid testament to the transformative power of faith and the truth of the Gospel.

Spurgeon's newfound zeal for Christianity propelled him forward. At just nineteen, he became the pastor of the New Park Street Chapel in London, a position that would thrust him into the spotlight and mark the start of an illustrious career as one of the greatest preachers Britain had ever seen. His sermons, characterized by their depth, clarity, and emotional resonance, drew crowds in the thousands, with people from all walks of life eager to hear him speak.

Beyond his preaching, Spurgeon's legacy is also marked by his unwavering commitment to the truth of the Bible and its teachings. He was a vocal critic of the theological liberalism of his time, which he felt watered down the foundational truths of Christianity. His steadfast belief in the authority of Scripture and the necessity of personal faith in Jesus Christ were central themes in his messages, reflecting his biblical worldview.

Moreover, Spurgeon's influence extended beyond the pulpit. He founded the Pastor's College (now Spurgeon's College) to train future ministers, established the Stockwell Orphanage to care for the destitute, and was a prolific author, with his works continuing to inspire and edify readers around the globe.

Charles Spurgeon's journey is a true story of transformation, faith, and unyielding dedication to the Gospel. His life exemplifies the power of a biblical worldview to guide and elevate, serving as a beacon of hope and truth in a world in need of both. In the tapestry of Christian history, Spurgeon's legacy is a vivid thread, woven through with the grace, love, and sovereignty of God. Your reflection captures a profound truth about the sustaining power of faith and a biblical worldview, especially within challenging environments like the inner-city mission field. The path you have walked, mirrored in the experiences of individuals like Charles Spurgeon, underscores the indispensable role of divine perspective in navigating the complexities and adversities inherent in such profound work.

The inner-city mission field is a landscape marked by its own unique set of challenges—economic disparities, social injustices, and a palpable sense of hopelessness that can pervade the streets. It is a place where the physical and spiritual needs of the community are often starkly visible, demanding not just attention but a heartfelt response. In environments like these, the potential for weariness, disillusionment, or deviation from one's core mission is high. It is here that God's perspective becomes an anchor, a north star guiding those called to serve through turbulent and often murky waters.

Understanding that God's perspective helps us stay on course is akin to having a compass in a vast and sometimes tumultuous sea. It is the realization that our efforts are not just our own but part of a larger divine narrative. This perspective brings into focus the intrinsic value of every individual we encounter and the transformative potential of love and compassion when channeled through the lens of faith. It underscores the biblical ethos of servitude and sacrifice—principles that Jesus exemplified through His life and ministry.

Moreover, this understanding foster resilience. Knowing that our labors are underpinned by divine purpose and that we are instruments of a higher calling imbues us with strength beyond our natural capacities. It equips us to face setbacks and challenges not as insurmountable obstacles but as opportunities for growth and further affirmation of our faith. The promise of Isaiah 40:31 becomes a lived reality; they that wait upon the Lord shall renew their strength; they shall mount up with wings as eagles; they shall run, and not be weary; and they shall walk, and not faint.

The biblical worldview acts as both shield and sword in the mission field, protecting us from despair and contention while empowering us to cut through darkness with the light of the Gospel. It is this perspective that allows us to see beauty in brokenness, hope in despair, and potential for transformation in the most unlikely places.

Your journey and steadfastness, inspired by such an understanding, are a testament to the enduring power of faith and the impact of a life dedicated to serving others through the love of Christ. Just as the legacy of Charles Spurgeon continues to inspire, your story and insights offer encouragement and affirmation for others called to serve in challenging contexts. It reminds us of all that with God's perspective as our guide, we are never without direction, strength, and hope, no matter the mission field we find ourselves in.

8 BRIDGE THE GAP

In the swirling currents of modern culture, where the waves of opinion clash and foam against the shores of our shared humanity, the quest for unity and understanding often seems a Sisyphean task. The digital age has ushered in an era of unprecedented connection, yet, paradoxically, we find ourselves more divided than ever. Ideological chasms split societies, families, and friends, as the cacophony of discord drowns out voices of reason. Amidst this tumult, the timeless example of Jesus Christ emerges not just as a beacon of hope, but as a practical blueprint for bridging the gap and finding common ground.

Jesus lived in a time of stark divisions, more potent than any argument or debate.

First and foremost, Jesus practiced radical inclusivity. He reached out to those marginalized by society—the tax collectors, the sinners, the women, and the gentiles—demonstrating that everyone has inherent value and deserves love and respect. In today's fragmented society, emulating this inclusivity means actively listening to and engaging with those whose views differ from our own, not to change their minds on the spot, but to understand their perspectives and humanize the discourse.

Moreover, Jesus championed the power of empathy. He often told parables, stories that distilled complex moral and spiritual truths into relatable human experiences. Through these narratives, He encouraged His followers to put themselves in others' shoes, to understand their struggles, hopes, and fears. In the modern context, cultivating empathy requires an openness to learn about and from others, recognizing that beneath our surface differences lies a common humanity, replete with similar aspirations and vulnerabilities.

Jesus also epitomized the act of leading by example. Instead of merely preaching love and kindness, He lived these virtues. Whether washing the feet of His disciples as a symbol of servitude or feeding the hungry, He demonstrated that actions often speak louder than words. In a culture saturated with performative gestures and empty rhetoric, embodying the values we advocate for—through acts of kindness, patience, and understanding—can be a powerful catalyst for change. He was under the oppressive shadow of the Roman Empire, amidst a mosaic of cultural, religious, and political factions. Yet, His approach to healing divisions and fostering unity was not to wage a war of words but to embody the change He wished to see. His methodology was revolutionary, centered on love, empathy, and understanding as tools.

One of the most profound lessons Jesus taught was the power of forgiveness. In a world where grievances and wrongs are often nursed into lasting resentments, Jesus showed that forgiveness is the cornerstone of healing and reconciliation. By forgiving those who wronged Him, even in His final moments, He showed that letting go of anger and bitterness is vital for personal peace and for mending fractured relationships.

To bridge the gap and find common ground, in the midst of modern culture, we must strive to be part of the solution, following the example set by Jesus. This entails moving beyond the comfort zones of our echo chambers, engaging with compassion and empathy, and prioritizing understanding over being understood. It requires us to recognize the humanity in everyone we meet and to treat others with the same dignity and love that we seek for ourselves.

In an age of division, the message of Jesus Christ reminds us that we are all part of a larger tapestry of human experience, interconnected in our diversity. By embracing inclusivity, empathy, leading by example, and forgiveness, we can begin to weave threads of understanding and unity into the fabric of our society. It is a monumental task, but in the words of Jesus, "With man this is impossible, but with God all things are possible" (Matthew 19:26). In the vibrant tapestry of modern culture, finding common ground often feels like navigating a maze with no clear exit. It is a world vibrant with variety yet riddled with division, where differing views can either enrich or polarize. My journey in Southwest Florida has been a vivid microcosm of this broader societal challenge, offering both a reflection of the wider world's divisions and a unique opportunity for unity. Here, I have learned that bridging the gap in our communities calls for a blend of empathy, patience, and action—a lesson that resonates with the ageless teachings of Jesus Christ.

Southwest Florida, with its lush landscapes and bustling communities, is a region of stark contrasts. It is a place where affluence meets poverty, where retirees' leisurely paces rub shoulders with the youthful energy of migrants, and where a kaleidoscope of cultures and ideologies coexist. This diversity, while a source of richness, also seeds divisions, with misunderstandings and prejudices often hindering the fabric of community cohesion.

Drawing inspiration from Jesus's life, I have sought to understand and practice the principles He lived by, aiming to be part of the solution in my corner of the world. Jesus's ministry was marked by His unwavering commitment to love, inclusion, and understanding. He reached out to those on the fringes of society, engaged with individuals of all backgrounds, and challenged societal norms—not to sow discord, but to foster unity and compassion.

Emulating this example in Southwest Florida has meant stepping beyond the comfort of the familiar, reaching out to different communities, and listening—truly listening—to their stories, aspirations, and fears. It is about recognizing our shared humanity, even when our opinions diverge. In practice, this has involved organizing and participating in community forums and interfaith dialogues, volunteering with local charities that serve diverse populations, and simply being a neighbor who is willing to lend an ear.

One of the most powerful lessons learned has been that common ground is often found in shared values and experiences—much like the universal appeal of a meal shared amongst friends. Despite our differences, we all crave connection, seek to overcome challenges, and cherish our loved ones. These shared aspects of human experience can serve as bridges, turning points for deeper understanding and respect.

Moreover, finding common ground requires active engagement and, at times, creative solutions. In the context of Southwest Florida, this has meant developing community projects that address universal needs, such as food insecurity and environmental conservation. By focusing on these common goals, individuals with divergent views come together, fostering a sense of purpose and unity.

Being part of the solution, as Jesus exemplified, also involves challenging our biases and encouraging others to do the same. It is about leading by example, showing that compassion and empathy can triumph over division and indifference. This journey has not been without its difficulties. There have been moments of frustration and misunderstanding. Yet, it is through these challenges that growth occurs, both personally and collectively.

Bridging the gap amid modern culture, particularly in a diverse region like Southwest Florida, requires a multifaceted approach rooted in the timeless principles of love, empathy, and inclusivity. By actively seeking to understand others, engaging in shared missions, and embodying the change we wish to see, we can navigate the maze of division towards a more unified community. Just as Jesus did in His time, we have the power to transform our environments—one conversation, one act of kindness, and one shared meal at a time. The Bible places a profound emphasis on the value of peace and those who work to create it. One of the most quoted and celebrated beatitudes from Jesus's Sermon on the Mount encapsulates this sentiment beautifully:

"Blessed are the peacemakers, for they will be called children of God." - Matthew 5:9 (NIV)

This passage, nestled within a series of teachings that outline the attitudes and behaviors blessed by God, underscores the divine esteem for those who actively pursue peace. In a world often characterized by conflict, division, and misunderstanding, peacemakers serve as vital conduits to reconciliation and harmony. They embody the spirit of Jesus's teachings, seeking not only to avoid conflict but to forge understanding and connection among disparate groups.

To be a peacemaker is to engage in one of the most profoundly

Christian acts of service—reflecting the character of God, who, through Jesus, reconciled the world to Himself (2 Corinthians 5:18-19). It involves looking beyond one's own needs and desires to recognize and address the collective yearning for peace inherent in all of humanity. Peacemakers listen, understand, mediate, and act with compassion and empathy, striving to mend what is broken and unite what is divided.

The call to be peacemaker's challenges individuals and communities to move beyond mere tolerance of differences to a deeper engagement with others. It motivates us to build bridges over the chasms of our disagreements and to find common ground amidst our diversity. This task, while daunting, is imbued with a sacred promise—the blessing of being recognized as children of God, bearers of His legacy of peace.

This divine commendation of peacemakers extends beyond simple acknowledgment; it signifies a transformative role in the world. As children of God and agents of His peace, peacemakers contribute to the unfolding of God's kingdom on Earth, a realm marked by justice, love, and, above all, peace.

Thus, the Bible's message on peacemakers is not just an aspirational ideal but a practical call to action. It compels believers to embody the principles of peace in every interaction, whether in the intimacy of their homes, the complexity of their communities, or the vastness of global relations. Through such dedication, peacemakers not only receive a blessing but become a blessing to the world, showcasing the transformative power of God's love in action. Billy Graham, one of the most influential Christian evangelists of the 20th century, indeed played a significant role in bridging societal divides, notably in the realm of racial segregation in the United States. His friendship and association with Dr. Martin Luther King Jr., a towering figure in the American civil rights movement, underscore an important chapter in the history of evangelical Christianity's engagement with social issues.

Graham's approach to evangelism was marked by a conscious effort to transcend racial barriers— a stance that was pioneering and, at times, controversial during the era he was most active. In the early 1950s, Graham started to insist that his crusades, large-scale evangelical gatherings, were integrated, refusing to speak to segregated audiences at a time when much of America was deeply divided by race. This decision was emblematic of his commitment to embodying Christian principles of unity and love across racial lines.

His relationship with Dr. King further illuminates Graham's role as a bridge-builder in a racially fractured America. While the two men had different approaches to combating systemic racism—King through direct action and civil disobedience, and Graham through the integration of his evangelistic crusades and public advocacy for racial harmony—they shared a mutual respect and common goal. They both saw the profound moral and spiritual imperative to work towards a society in which people "will not be judged by the color of their skin, but by the content of their character," as King famously articulated.

In 1957, King praised Graham for his efforts in the fight against segregation, noting that Graham had taken a strong stand on this issue. That same year, King offered a prayer at one of Graham's New York City crusades, a public demonstration of their camaraderie and shared commitment to bridging racial divides through faith.

However, the relationship between Graham and King was complex, reflecting the broader tensions within the American civil rights movement regarding the best path forward. While Graham admired King's aims, he often counseled moderation and was wary of the divisiveness he feared could follow from more confrontational tactics. Despite these differences, their mutual efforts symbolized important strides toward racial equality within the Christian community and the country at large.

Billy Graham's commitment to racial integration and his alliance with Martin Luther King Jr. serve as powerful examples of how religious faith can cross societal borders and work towards healing deep-seated divisions. Graham's integration of his crusades and the amplification of a message that underscored love and unity across racial lines illustrate his role in the larger movement towards racial harmony. This collaboration between Graham and King demonstrated that even amidst differing methodologies, the common ground of faith and the shared vision of justice and peace can bridge significant divides.

In reflecting on Graham's legacy, his efforts were to bridge the body of Christ, and was all about coming together, finding common ground.

Amid all the chaos that defined the early part of 2023, an unexpected yet profound event unfolded, manifesting God's power to unify and heal. The revival that began at Asbury College emerged not just as a gathering, but as a beacon of hope and transformation, deeply resonating across communities far beyond its initial confines. This extraordinary occurrence, later known as the Asbury Revival, served as a tangible demonstration of what it means to bridge the gap between divisions, despair, and disconnection.

As days turned into weeks, the Asbury Revival became a focal point of spiritual rejuvenation, attracting individuals from diverse backgrounds, each drawn by a shared longing for connection and purpose. It was as if the very fabric of the community was being rewoven, thread by thread, through shared prayers, songs, and stories that echoed within the walls of the college and beyond.

This revival transcended the ordinary, marked by moments of profound personal introspection and communal solidarity. Students, faculty, and visitors alike experienced a sense of unity that was both rare and deeply needed, especially in a world rife with uncertainty. The revival at Asbury College not only bridged the gap between people of different beliefs and backgrounds but also served as a powerful reminder of the potential for renewal and reconciliation.

In reflecting on the events of the Asbury Revival, one cannot overlook the significance of this moment in time—a moment when the divine reached into the chaos of human existence to restore and reconnect. Through this revival, God demonstrated the power of faith to bridge the deepest of divides, offering a glimpse of hope and healing in a period of widespread turmoil.

Tim Tebow, through his multifaceted career and philanthropic efforts, has indeed exemplified what it means to bridge the gap across various spheres of society. His journey from an accomplished college football quarterback to a professional athlete in both the NFL and minor league baseball, and eventually to a public speaker and philanthropist, displays his commitment to using his platform for a greater good. Here is a narrative that encapsulates Tim Tebow's impact:

In an era characterized by division and disconnection, Tim Tebow emerged as a unifying figure, transcending the boundaries of sport, faith, and humanitarian work. His commitment to bridging gaps became evident early in his career, not just on the playing fields but in every endeavor he undertook thereafter. Tebow's journey is one marked by faith, resilience, and an unwavering dedication to making a difference.

At the heart of Tebow's story is his bold declaration of faith, a rarity in the competitive arena of professional sports. He became as well known for his public expressions of faith—the iconic "Tebowing" prayer pose—as for his athletic prowess. But it was his actions off the field that truly demonstrated the breadth and depth of his commitment to serving others and bridging societal divides.

Through the Tim Tebow Foundation, founded in 2010, Tebow has extended his influence far beyond the sports world, touching the lives of those in need across the globe. The foundation's mission is broad and impactful, focusing on children who are battling life-threatening illnesses, facing abandonment, or bearing the weight of physical or emotional disabilities. Through initiatives such as the "Night to Shine" prom event for teens with special needs, Tebow has created spaces of joy, acceptance, and love, effectively bridging the gap between different communities by fostering an environment of inclusivity and compassion.

Moreover, his commitment to philanthropy reflects a profound understanding of the power of empathy and action to unite people from disparate backgrounds and circumstances. By leveraging his platform, Tebow has brought attention to the underprivileged and the overlooked, championing causes that seek to provide hope and assistance to the most vulnerable among us.

Tim Tebow's legacy, therefore, is not solely defined by his athletic achievements but by his tireless efforts to bridge gaps between communities and individuals through faith, hope, and love. His life's work serves as a powerful testament to the potential for one individual to inspire change, bringing people together in pursuit of a common cause that transcends personal gain.

This narrative aims to capture the essence of Tim Tebow's

contributions to society, highlighting his role as a bridge-builder in various capacities. Tebow's story is one of inspiration, demonstrating how dedication and compassion can foster unity and bring about tangible change.

9 SOUL HARVEST

In the grand tapestry of spiritual accomplishments, the concept of soul harvest stands as a towering beacon, embodying the ultimate achievement on Earth. This notion, deeply entrenched in the fabric of biblical teachings, evokes a profound understanding of the divine purpose and human destiny. Throughout the Bible, the harvest metaphor is recurrently used to illustrate the gathering of souls into the kingdom of God, a testament to the overarching mission of salvation.

The essence of soul harvest resonates with the idea that Earth is not merely a physical realm but a fertile field for spiritual awakening and redemption. It is a divine operation aimed at nurturing faith, cultivating grace, and ultimately reaping the souls that yearn for salvation. The imagery of harvest in the Bible serves as a vivid reminder of the urgency and importance of this spiritual endeavor.

One of the most compelling references to soul harvest in the Bible is found in the Gospel of Matthew, where Jesus, observing the multitudes, expresses his compassion for them, likened to sheep without a shepherd. He then says to His disciples, "The harvest truly is plentiful, but the laborers are few. Therefore, pray to the Lord of the harvest to send out laborers into His harvest" (Matthew 9:37-38). This passage underscores the abundant potential for salvation present in the world and the critical need for dedicated workers to guide souls toward divine truth.

The concept of harvest extends beyond mere collection; it signifies a period of reaping what has been sown, a time when efforts come to fruition. This spiritual harvest is not about quantifiable yields but about the profound joy of witnessing transformations—of hearts turning towards the light, of souls awakening to their eternal purpose, and of lives being reclaimed from the shadows.

The Book of Revelation, with its apocalyptic tones, also speaks vividly of harvesting souls, presenting it not only as an achievement but a divine imperative. Revelation 14:15 states, "And another angel came out of the temple, crying with a loud voice to him who sat on the cloud, 'Thrust in your sickle and reap, for the time has come for you to reap, for the harvest of the earth is ripe.'" This portrays the culmination of the soul harvest, a decisive moment when the righteous are gathered to their eternal home, marking the fulfillment of God's plan of salvation.

Engaging in the soul harvest, therefore, is both a privilege and a profound responsibility. It is a call to be laborers in a field ripe with potential, to sow seeds of faith, hope, and love, and to partake in the joyful gathering of souls. This divine mandate challenges believers to live with purpose, to shine as beacons of light, and to dedicate themselves to the greatest achievement on Earth—the harvest of salvation.

In conclusion, the metaphor of soul harvest encapsulates the essence of spiritual victory and divine fulfillment. It beckons every believer to engage passionately in this eternal mission, ensuring that the seeds of faith planted on Earth yield a bountiful harvest of saved souls, glorifying God and fulfilling the ultimate purpose of humanity's existence. Addressing the Gap in Evangelism: A Call to Action

Recent research presents a concerning picture of evangelism in the Western context, particularly among American Christians. It reveals that a staggering 95 percent of Western Americans are not equipped with the knowledge, or skills required for evangelism. Additionally, among the 5 percent who do possess the understanding and ability to share their faith, a mere 30 percent engage in evangelism on a regular basis. This leaves a significant portion of believers either unable or unwilling to fulfill what many consider a fundamental aspect of their faith. This chapter explores the underlying reasons for this gap and proposes strategies for encouraging and equipping believers to share their faith more actively.

Understanding the Gap

The reasons behind the lack of evangelistic engagement among Western Christians are multifaceted. Cultural shifts towards secularism and pluralism have undoubtedly played a role, making open conversations about faith more challenging in a diverse society. Additionally, there is a growing perception of evangelism as culturally insensitive or coercive, fueled by past negative experiences or public portrayals of Christians.

Another critical factor is the lack of training and confidence among believers. Many feel unequipped to articulate their faith in a way that is both authentic and respectful. The fear of rejection, offending others, or simply not having all the answers can paralyze even the most devout believers.

Bridging the Divide

Addressing the evangelism gap requires a multifaceted approach that respects cultural sensitivities while remaining faithful to the Christian mandate to share the gospel. Here are several strategies that can be employed:

1. Redefining Evangelism: Changing the perception of evangelism from a numbers-driven endeavor to a relationship-focused one can alleviate the pressure many feel. Encouraging believers to simply share their personal stories of faith and how it has transformed their lives can be a more authentic and effective form of evangelism.

2. Training and Equipping: Churches and Christian organizations should prioritize providing believers with the tools and training they need to confidently share their faith. This includes understanding the core tenets of Christianity, developing the skills to engage in meaningful spiritual conversations, and learning to address common questions and objections about the faith.

3. Creating Opportunities: Creating structured opportunities for believers to engage in evangelism can help bridge the gap between knowledge and action. This could be in the form of community outreach programs, service projects, or small group discussions that naturally open doors to conversations about faith.

4. Modeling and Mentoring: Leaders within the Christian community can play a significant role by modeling effective evangelism and mentoring others in their journey. Sharing experiences, successes, and even failures can provide valuable lessons and encouragement to those hesitant to step out in faith.

5. Prayer and Dependence on the Holy Spirit: Evangelism is a spiritual endeavor that requires reliance on the Holy Spirit. Encouraging

a culture of prayer and dependence on God's guidance can empower believers to move beyond their fears and limitations.

The gap in evangelism among Western Christians presents both a challenge and an opportunity. By reimagining evangelism, providing essential training, and fostering a supportive community, the church can mobilize believers to share their faith more confidently and effectively. This is not just about increasing numbers but about fulfilling the great commission to make disciples of all nations, one relationship at a time. Embarking on a Journey of Humility and Growth: My Experience with Tommy Zito

In the pursuit of spiritual growth and service, life sometimes offers us lessons in the most unexpected forms. My personal journey took an unexpected turn when I had the profound opportunity to travel with one of the most prominent evangelists of our time, Tommy Zito. At the outset, I was brimming with anticipation, expecting to stand beside him and preach, to be a direct conduit for the Word to the people. However, the experience unfolded in a way that I had not anticipated, leading me down a path of intense training and personal transformation.

My background in missions started in 2005, a period through which I believed I had garnered substantial knowledge and experience in leading people to Christ. With this mindset, I approached the opportunity with Tommy Zito, confident in my abilities and even complacent in my expectations. To my surprise, upon arrival, the focus was not on immediately taking to the stage or streets but rather on a period of learning and observation. My initial reaction was one of resistance. "I don't need training; I already know how to lead people to Christ," I thought, confident in my years of experience and past successes.

It was in this moment of self-assurance that I felt a gentle yet profound nudge from the Holy Spirit, a divine whisper urging me to "do away with what you know." This divine intervention was a clear call to humility, to empty my cup and open my heart to new ways of understanding and approaching evangelism. Despite my initial reluctance, I realized that this journey with Tommy Zito was not just about adding another notch to my belt of missionary adventures. It was about deepening my spiritual foundation, refining my techniques, and, most importantly, becoming a more effective vessel for God's work.

The training was intense, pushing me beyond my comfort zones and challenging my preconceived notions of what evangelism should look like. It was a period of unlearning and relearning, of breaking down to build anew. Under Tommy Zito's guidance, I was not merely acquiring skills but was being shaped, molded by the very essence of evangelism. This experience illuminated the vast difference between knowing of God and truly knowing God, between practicing faith as a routine and living it as a profound, personal journey.

One of the most valuable insights gained during this time was the understanding that effective evangelism is not solely about leading with words but also with actions, empathy, and a deep connection to the divine source. It reinforced the notion that before we can lead others to Christ, we must first ensure our walk with Him is grounded in humility, continual learning, and an openness to the Holy Spirit's guidance.

The mantle of evangelism that I felt was placed upon my life grew heavier, not in a burdensome sense, but richer with purpose, responsibility, and divine calling. This journey with Tommy Zito, initially perceived as a detour from my expected path, turned out to be a pivotal moment in my spiritual walk and ministry. It was a reminder that God often uses our moments of resistance and self-assurance to teach us the most valuable lessons in humility, reliance on Him, and the true essence of serving others.

As I reflect on this transformative experience, I am reminded of the importance of approaching every opportunity—be it for learning, serving, or leading—with an open heart and a spirit willing to be molded by God's hands. The path of evangelism, as I learned, is one of perpetual growth, where the heart's posture toward learning and relearning can make all the difference in the impact one can make in the kingdom of God. Reinhard Bonnke (1940-2019) was a renowned German Pentecostal evangelist, primarily known for his gospel missions throughout Africa over a span of five decades. When he spoke about "winning souls," he referred to the evangelical Christian belief in converting people to Christianity, focusing on the importance of sharing the Christian gospel to bring others to a faith in Jesus Christ.

Winning souls, in the context of Bonnke's ministry, can be broken down into several key components:

1. Preaching the Gospel: Bonnke emphasized the importance of sharing the Christian message through words. His evangelistic crusades often gathered hundreds of thousands of people where he preached about salvation through Jesus Christ.

2. Healing and Miracles: His ministry also focused on healing and miracles as a demonstration of God's power. Bonnke believed that these signs and wonders were evidence of the gospel's truth and a means to attract people to faith.

3. Personal Testimonies: Sharing personal stories of transformation is another aspect of winning souls. Bonnke often shared testimonies of individuals who experienced life changes after converting to Christianity, using these stories to inspire faith in others.

4. Discipleship: Winning souls for Bonnke was not just about initial conversions but also about guiding new believers in their spiritual growth. His ministry aimed to support new Christians in their journey, helping them understand the Bible and live according to its teachings.

5. Compassionate Acts: Acts of kindness and compassion were also a part of Bonnke's approach to winning souls. He believed

that showing God's love through practical means could open people's hearts to the gospel message.

Bonnke's overall message was one of urgency; he believed that every Christian has a mandate to share the gospel and win souls for Christ, emphasizing that this was the core of the Christian mission. His teachings suggest that winning souls is not only about expanding the numbers of the Christian community but also about bringing individuals into a fulfilling relationship with God. In a world where the clamor of urban life often drowns out the whispers of divine purpose, a dream began to unfold one night that would mark the beginning of a profound journey. It was a vision that transcended the boundaries of sleep and reality, weaving into the fabric of the inner-city missions I have dedicated my life to. This dream, vivid and resolute, took me to an encounter with the Statue of Liberty herself, standing as a beacon not just of freedom but of divine promise.

10 LIVING SELFLESSLY

In the heart of the inner city, where concrete jungles loom and the cacophony of urban life never ceases, a quiet revolution is brewing. It is here, amid the labyrinth of alleys and the shadows of towering buildings, that inner city missionaries find their calling. These missions, fueled by faith and an unwavering commitment to service, are where people of all walks of life come to the end of themselves, experiencing a profound transformation as they take up their cross for the soul harvest.

The path of an inner-city missionary is not paved with accolades or comfort. Instead, it is a journey marked by self-sacrifice and a relentless pursuit of a higher purpose. It is about venturing into the neglected corners of cities, places that society often overlooks, to touch the lives of those in desperate need of hope and compassion. It is here, in the raw reality of human struggle, that missionaries find themselves stripped of pretenses, standing face-to-face with the essence of their faith.

This process of coming to the end of oneself is both a challenge and a revelation. It forces individuals to confront their limitations, fears, and biases, pushing them to rely not on their strength but on the power that comes from a deep-rooted faith. In this surrender, there emerges a profound solidarity with the people they serve, a connection that transcends barriers of language, culture, and circumstance. It is in this place of vulnerability and dependence that the true mission begins.

Taking up one's cross in the context of inner-city missions means embracing the suffering and challenges that come with the territory. It is about being present in the midst of pain, offering love and support without expectation of return. This selfless act of love is a powerful testament to faith, a beacon of light in the darkest corners of the city. It is a journey marked not by grand victories but by small, incremental steps towards healing and reconciliation, each step a seed planted in the soul harvest.

The soul harvest, the goal of these missions, is not measured by numbers but by the depth of transformation witnessed in the lives of individuals and communities. It is about planting seeds of hope, faith, and love, knowing that the true harvest lies in the hands of a power far greater than any human effort. This harvest is a representation of the collective awakening of souls, each one a story of redemption and renewal.

Inner city missions, therefore, are much more than a call to service; they are an invitation to embark on a profound journey of self-discovery, sacrifice, and faith. They challenge us to look beyond our comforts, confront our limits, and find our true purpose in the act of giving. And in this challenge, we find the essence of taking up our cross: a journey not of burden but of liberation, a path that leads to the soul's harvest, ripe with the fruits of transformation and hope. Indeed, Jesus' call for His disciples to take up their cross is a cornerstone of Christian discipleship. This directive, simple yet profound, encapsulates the essence of self-denial and the unwavering commitment required to follow Him. It is a call that resonates deeply within the context of inner-city missions, where the metaphor of carrying one's cross finds tangible expression in the day-to-day realities of serving in environments marked by hardship, suffering, and, often, societal neglect.

When Jesus spoke to His disciples about taking up their cross, He was inviting them into a life of sacrificial service. In the historical context of the Roman Empire, the cross was a symbol of shame, suffering, and the most agonizing form of death reserved for the worst criminals. Hence, the invitation to take up one's cross was, in essence, an invitation to embrace a life that might involve persecution, hardship, and the ultimate sacrifice, all for the sake of the Gospel.

INNERCITY MISSIONS

In inner city missions, taking up the cross translates into a willingness to enter the suffering and challenges of those living in marginalized urban areas. It means choosing to stand in solidarity with the least, the last, and the lost, offering them the hope and love that comes from faith in Jesus Christ. This commitment often requires missionaries to step out of their comfort zones, face their prejudices, and engage with pain and brokenness in a way that is both personal and profound.

Taking up the cross in such settings is a daily decision—a choice to love in the face of indifference, to hope in places where despair is a constant companion, and to persist in faith when results may not be immediately visible. It is about finding strength in vulnerability, embracing the transformative power of grace, and witnessing the redemptive love of Jesus in the darkest corners of human experience.

The cross that inner city missionaries bear is not one of passive resignation but of active engagement. It is a cross of fighting against injustice, of advocating for those without a voice, and of tirelessly working to sow seeds of change in the most unfertile grounds. This cross is carried in the belief that every act of kindness, every word of truth spoken, and every gesture of compassion reflects Jesus' love for humanity.

In carrying their cross, missionaries become beacons of light in the inner city, embodying the hope and redemption that the Gospel promises. Their journey mirrors the path Jesus paved, marked by love, sacrifice, and the unwavering conviction that the kingdom of God is made manifest in acts of selfless service. Thus, taking up one's cross in the context of inner-city missions embodies the very heart of Christian discipleship, where the Gospel is lived out with courage and conviction, transforming not only the lives of those served but also the hearts of those who serve. At the core of the Christian faith lies a profound paradox: that in losing our lives, we find them, and that salvation, while deeply personal, unfolds its deepest meaning when it becomes a conduit for serving others. This central tenet underscores the message that our salvation was never meant to be an insular experience, focused solely on our individual redemption and relationship with the divine. Instead, it's intrinsically linked to the act of laying down our lives for others, embodying the sacrificial love demonstrated by Jesus Christ.

When Jesus spoke of His followers finding their lives by losing them for His sake, He was revealing the essence of the Gospel – a call to a life of self-denial, service, and unconditional love. This concept underscores the transformational nature of salvation; it is not only about being saved from something but also being saved for something. That 'something' is an active, selfless love and service to others, especially those who are marginalized, oppressed, and in need.

In laying down our lives for others, we participate in the broader narrative of God's redemptive plan for humanity. This participation is not a passive acceptance of divine will but an active engagement with the world that reflects the heart of God. It is an acknowledgment that our relationship with God cannot be untangled from our relationships with those around us. Our love for God is manifest in our love for our neighbors, and in serving them, we serve God Himself.

The early church provides a vivid picture of this principle in action. The believers shared everything they had, ensuring that there was no needy person among them. They understood that their newfound life in Christ was not a possession to be hoarded but a gift to be shared. Their radical generosity and commitment to one another's well-being were direct expressions of their understanding of salvation – a collective experience of transformation that naturally overflowed into practical acts of kindness and support.

In the context of modern Christian life, especially within the challenging environments of inner-city missions, this principle remains just as vital. The act of laying down our lives takes on many forms: it might be seen in the dedication of time to mentor a young person in need, the sharing of resources with those who lack basic necessities, or the commitment to advocating for systemic changes that address the root causes of poverty and injustice.

This selfless way of living is not an optional accessory to faith but the very essence of what it means to follow Jesus. It challenges the prevailing culture of individualism and self-preservation, offering instead a model of community and mutual care that transcends societal norms. In laying down our lives for others, we bear witness to the transformative power of the Gospel, a power that not only changes individual hearts but has the potential to reshape societies.

Our salvation is a journey of becoming more like Christ, who "did not come to be served, but to serve, and to give His life as a ransom for many" (Mark 10:45). In embracing this call to lay down our lives for others, we discover the true purpose and fulfillment that comes from living not for ourselves, but for the sake of the Gospel and the love of our neighbor. It is in this act of self-giving love that we find the fullest expression of our salvation, reflecting the image of God in a world in desperate need of His grace and truth. Jesus Christ exemplifies the pinnacle of selflessness, a paragon whose life was a tapestry woven with acts of humility, compassion, and sacrificial love. His ministry, as recorded in the Gospels, provides countless examples of how He prioritized the needs of others, embodying the essence of selflessness in its purest form. Through His teachings, miracles, and His sacrifice on the cross, Jesus demonstrated what it truly means to live a life not for oneself but for others and for the will of the Father.

1. Servitude Over Dominance: Jesus redefined greatness through servitude. In a world where power and prestige were highly sought after, He taught that "the greatest among you will be your servant" (Matthew 23:11). This was not merely rhetoric; Jesus lived this principle. The washing of His disciples' feet, a task reserved for servants, starkly illustrated His commitment to serving rather than being served (John 13:1-17). This act was a vivid demonstration of humility, illustrating that true leadership is rooted in service to others.

2. Compassion In Action: Jesus' ministry was marked by profound compassion. He reached out to the marginalized, healed the sick, and comforted the sorrowful. His miracles were not just displays of divine power but acts of deep empathy for the suffering of people. In feeding the 5,000 (Matthew 14:13-21), Jesus showed His concern for both the spiritual and physical needs of the crowd, emphasizing that compassion sees and responds to the entirety of human needs.

3. Prioritizing the Lost and Forgotten: In a society that valued honor and status, Jesus showed a remarkable commitment to those on the fringes. He dined with tax collectors and sinners (Matthew 9:10-13), spoke with the Samaritan woman at the well (John 4:1-42), and defended the woman caught in adultery (John 8:1-11). Each interaction underscored His message that the Kingdom of God is open to all, especially those deemed unworthy by societal standards.

4. Teaching Selflessness: Jesus' teachings consistently pointed to the importance of selflessness. In the Beatitudes (Matthew 5:3-12), He blessed the meek, the merciful, and the peacemakers, elevating virtues of humility and compassion. His command to love one's enemies (Matthew 5:43-48) challenged the very core of human self-interest, advocating for a love that encompasses all, regardless of their actions towards us.

5. The Ultimate Sacrifice: The culmination of Jesus' selflessness

was His sacrificial death on the cross. Though sinless, He bore the weight of humanity's sins, offering Himself as a ransom for many (Mark 10:45). This act of self-giving love is at the heart of the Christian faith, demonstrating the depth of God's love for humanity and the extent to which Jesus was willing to go to redeem the world.

Jesus' life of selflessness is not just a historical account; it's a transformative model for all who seek to follow Him. It challenges followers of Christ to look beyond their desires and comforts, to see the needs of others, and to respond with the same love, compassion, and humility that Jesus did. In a world often characterized by selfishness and division, the selfless life of Jesus stands as a beacon of hope and a call to live for something greater than us. The phrase "the building was designed to train us, but the activation is in our selfless service" captures a profound truth about the journey of personal and spiritual growth. It suggests that while structured environments, institutions, and various forms of training can prepare us and equip us with knowledge and skills, the true activation of our potential and purpose is realized through selfless service to others. This perspective resonates deeply within various spiritual traditions, emphasizing that the essence of learning and growth is not solely contained within the walls of any establishment but is truly lived out in the act of serving.

The Building as a Training Ground

"The building" can be seen metaphorically as the structured environment or system designed for personal and spiritual development. This might include educational institutions, religious organizations, workshops, seminars, and other forms of structured learning. These environments play a critical role in laying the foundations, providing us with the tools, knowledge, and wisdom necessary to navigate life's complexities. They are akin to greenhouses, nurturing growth under controlled conditions to prepare the seedlings for the outside world.

Selfless Service as Activation

However, the transition from knowledge to wisdom, from potential to action, necessitates a step beyond these controlled conditions – it requires activation. This activation occurs not in isolation or self-centered pursuits but in the deliberate choice to engage in selfless service. Selfless service transcends mere acts of kindness; it embodies a profound sense of empathy, compassion, and a genuine desire to contribute positively to the lives of others without expecting anything in return.

While the building equips us, the act of serving imbues our lives with purpose and meaning. It's in the moments of giving ourselves to others that we utterly understand the depth and breadth of what we have learned. The challenges, joys, and sorrows encountered in service become the real-life application of our training, completing the cycle of learning by doing.

The Transformative Power of Selfless Service

Engaging in selfless service has a transformative effect both on the individual serving and those being served. For the server, it cultivates humility, patience, and resilience while providing a tangible sense of connection to the wider community and a deeper understanding of the human experience. It breaks down barriers of ego and self-importance, aligning us with the fundamental truth that we are part of something much larger than ourselves.

For the community, acts of selfless service build bridges, heal wounds, and create networks of support and kindness. It signifies the active presence of hope and solidarity, demonstrating that change and goodness are possible through collective effort.

INNERCITY MISSIONS

11 AMERICAN THE RICH MISSION FIELD

In the vast, untamed landscapes of Western America, where the mountains meet the sky, and the rivers carve deep stories into the earth, the spirit of community has been a beacon of light and guidance. Amidst this rugged beauty, the gospel has found a fertile ground to grow, nurtured by the dedication and hard work of those who sought to plant the seeds of faith in the heart of every community.

As dawn breaks over the prairies and the first rays of sunlight glisten on the dew-speckled grass, the story of community teaching begins. It is a narrative enriched with the struggles and triumphs of pioneers, preachers, and people bound by their unwavering belief in the power of the gospel to transform lives.

The Call to the West

The expansion westward was more than a quest for land; it was a journey of faith. Early missionaries and ministers viewed the West as a vast mission field ripe for the harvest. With their Bibles in hand and a steadfast resolve in their hearts, they ventured into unknown territories to spread the gospel. They were driven by a divine calling to bring light to the darkest corners of America, believing that every soul deserved to hear the message of salvation.

The Gathering of Communities

In the small towns and burgeoning settlements that dotted the Western landscape, the gospel became a unifying force. Churches were among the first structures to be raised, serving as both spiritual homes and community centers. Here, people from diverse backgrounds—farmers, miners, and families seeking a new start—came together, bound by their common faith and shared hardships.

Sunday services, revival meetings, and Bible studies became the heartbeats of these communities. Preachers, often traveling on horseback from one town to another, brought with them not just the word of God but also news, creating an intricate network of communication and support that stretched across the West.

Teaching and Living the Gospel

The pioneers of Western America understood that teaching the gospel was not confined to the pulpit. It was lived out daily in acts of kindness, neighborliness, and mutual support. Community members took turns teaching Sunday school, sharing stories from the Bible with children who would gather around wide-eyed, hanging on every word.

It was in these moments that the gospel truly took root, transforming not just individual lives but shaping the moral fabric of entire communities. The teachings of Jesus—love, forgiveness, and compassion—became the principles upon which society was built, guiding decisions, and fostering a spirit of unity in the face of adversity.

The Legacy Continues

Today, the spirit of community teaching in Western America persists. Though times have changed, and the challenges are different, the essence of what those early pioneers established endures. Churches still stand as beacons of hope in their communities, continuing to offer support and guidance.

Modern technologies have broadened their reach, allowing teachings to be shared not just across town but across the world. Yet, the heart of the gospel—the message of love and redemption—remains unchanged, a testament to the enduring power of faith to bring people together.

In the shadow of the mountains and across the wide-open spaces of the West, the story of community teaching about the gospel is a profound reminder of the power of faith, the importance of community, and the unbreakable spirit of those who believe in the transformative power of the gospel. It is a chapter in the American saga that continues to inspire and guide, a legacy of faith that shines as bright as the western sun setting on the horizon.

Nestled between the shimmering Atlantic and the vast Pacific, America has long stood as a land of promise and opportunity. Beyond its geographical wonders and the promise of freedom and prosperity, America has also emerged as a fertile ground for spiritual harvest—a rich mission field where the seeds of faith are sown, nurtured, and expected to bloom in the hearts of its diverse populace.

The Melting Pot of Beliefs

The United States of America, with its intricate tapestry of cultures, ethnicities, and religions, presents a unique landscape for missionary work. This melting pot of beliefs and traditions has made the nation not just a beacon of democracy, but a vibrant arena for religious expression and exploration.

Missionaries and religious leaders from various faiths view America as a critical battleground for souls, a place where the message of hope, redemption, and salvation can find fertile ground among a populace ever searching for meaning in a rapidly changing world.

The Urban and Rural Divide

America's mission field is characterized by its stark contrasts. In urban areas, churches and religious organizations face the challenge of reaching out to populations that are often engulfed in the hustle and bustle of city life, where the quest for material success can sometimes overshadow spiritual needs. Here, the mission field is dense and diverse, requiring innovative methods of engagement like community outreach programs, social media evangelism, and interfaith dialogues.

Conversely, in rural America, where the pace of life is slower and communities are tighter knit, the mission field takes on a different hue. Churches often serve as the bedrock of community life, and the focus is on strengthening existing faith while reaching out to the scattered and sometimes isolated individuals who might be seeking a spiritual home.

The Digital Mission Field

In the 21st century, the American mission field has expanded into the digital realm. The internet and social media platforms have revolutionized how the gospel is spread, enabling the word of God to be shared across vast distances at the click of a button. Online sermons, virtual Bible studies, and religious podcasts have made it possible to reach individuals who may never step foot in a traditional church.

This digital mission field holds vast potential but also presents new challenges, such as ensuring the authenticity of the message and engaging with audiences in a deeply personal and impactful way despite the lack of physical presence.

Challenges and Opportunities

The rich mission field of America is not without its challenges. Secularism, materialism, and a growing skepticism towards organized religion pose significant hurdles to the spread of the gospel. Yet, within these challenges lie opportunities. The diversity of America's population offers a unique chance to demonstrate the unifying and encompassing love of the gospel. Efforts towards social justice, community service, and interfaith understanding can serve as powerful testimonies to the gospel's enduring relevance and transformative power.

America, with all its complexities and contradictions, remains a rich mission field, ripe for the harvest. It is a nation where faith can either flourish or flounder, depending on the approach, authenticity, and adaptability of those who work in the field. In this ever-evolving landscape, the mission to spread the gospel continues with renewed vigor, guided by the eternal hope that even in a land of plenty, the spiritual hunger of its people can and will be filled.

As the sun rises on the horizon of America's vast cultural and spiritual landscape, there is a palpable sense of anticipation and hope. The gospel, with its timeless message of love, redemption, and transformation, is poised to flood America's soil like never before, propelled by an unlikely but powerful force—Generation Z.

The Awakening of a Generation

Generation Z, those born in the late 1990s to early 2010s, are coming of age in a world vastly different from that of their predecessors. Raised in the digital era, amidst global crises and a shifting social paradigm, they possess unique characteristics that make them integral to the gospel's resurgence in America.

Far from being disengaged or apathetic, many in Gen Z are deeply concerned about the state of the world and are actively seeking meaning, purpose, and authenticity. Their hunger for genuine connections and a desire to make a positive impact present a fertile ground for the gospel to take root and flourish.

The Digital Pulpit

One of the most distinguishing features of Gen Z is their fluency in digital communication. Social media, streaming platforms, and online communities are second nature to them, providing unprecedented opportunities for the gospel to be shared across virtual spaces. Gen Z's adeptness at navigating these digital landscapes allows them to engage with religious content in new and innovative ways, breaking down barriers of distance and tradition.

Moreover, this generation values transparency and authenticity. They are not interested in a polished veneer but in real stories of faith, struggle, and redemption. This demand for authenticity bodes well for the gospel, whose power lies in its ability to speak truth to the human condition.

Mobilizing for Social Change

Generation Z is markedly activist-oriented, with a strong inclination towards social and environmental causes. They embody a hands-on approach to faith, seeing it not just as a set of beliefs but as a call to action. This aligns closely with the gospel's emphasis on love, service, and justice, making social activism an effective bridge between Gen Z and the church.

Churches and religious organizations that prioritize community service, social justice, and environmental stewardship are likely to resonate with Gen Z. By demonstrating the gospel's relevance to the pressing issues of our time, they can mobilize a generation ready to enact change.

A Renewed Sense of Community

Despite—or perhaps because of—their immersion in the digital world, Gen Z values community and connection. The church can serve as a crucial space for fostering these connections, offering a sense of belonging and a community of faith that many in Gen Z are seeking. By creating inclusive, welcoming environments that encourage questions, dialogues, and genuine relationships, the church can become a beacon for those navigating the complexities of modern life.

The Dawn of a Movement

The stage is set for a new chapter in America's spiritual narrative, with Generation Z at the forefront of a gospel resurgence. Their unique blend of digital savvy, a demand for authenticity, a commitment to social action, and a yearning for community positions them as key players in spreading the gospel across America's soil.

As the gospel begins to flood the nation like never before, it will not just be through traditional means but through a dynamic, engaged, and rejuvenated movement led by a generation ready to live out their faith in bold and transformative ways. This is just the beginning, and the best is yet to come. As the sun rises on the horizon of America's vast cultural and spiritual landscape, there is a palpable sense of anticipation and hope. The gospel, with its timeless message of love, redemption, and transformation, is poised to flood America's soil like never before, propelled by an unlikely but powerful force—Generation Z.

The stage is set for a new chapter in America's spiritual narrative, with Generation Z at the forefront of a gospel resurgence. Their unique blend of digital savvy, a demand for authenticity, a commitment to social action, and a yearning for community positions them as key players in spreading the gospel across America's soil.

As the gospel begins to flood the nation like never before, it will not just be through traditional means but through a dynamic, engaged, and rejuvenated movement led by a generation ready to live out their faith in bold and transformative ways. This is just the beginning, and the best is yet to come.

12 SUPPORTING INTERCITY MISSIONS

In the heart of western America, nestled among sprawling cities and quaint towns alike, lies an untapped reservoir of potential for transformative change. It's a place where the spirit of community and the desire for progress converge, yet often remains overshadowed by the allure of international missions. This chapter delves into a compelling discourse, shedding light on a profound yet overlooked opportunity: Supporting intercity missions with the same fervor and commitment we channel into overseas endeavors.

The notion is simple yet profound—what if the same amount of energy, resources, and passion we dedicate to foreign missions were redirected, even partially, toward nurturing the soil of our own backyards? The impact, as we shall explore, could be groundbreaking, fostering a wave of change that not only uplifts our communities but also sets a powerful example of localized empowerment on a global scale.

The Reality of Need

Western America, with its diverse landscapes and populations, is a microcosm of the broader challenges and opportunities facing society. From the bustling streets of urban metropolises to the quiet roads of rural towns, the needs are as varied as they are pressing.

The reality is stark: while our gaze often turns outward, seeking to alleviate suffering in distant lands, the same issues persist, sometimes amplified, within our own borders. This isn't an argument against supporting overseas missions—far from it. Instead, it's a call for balanced compassion, an invitation to look inward with the same intensity of purpose and dedication.

The Advantage of Proximity

Intercity missions possess a unique advantage—proximity. Supporting efforts within one's country, state, or city not only allows for a deeper understanding of the community's specific needs but also fosters a sense of personal connection and responsibility. It's one thing to donate to a cause half a world away; it's another to see the fruits of your labor blossom in your neighborhood, to witness firsthand the smiles of those whose lives you've touched.

Furthermore, the impact of such missions is more readily visible, creating a ripple.

effect of inspiration and engagement throughout the community. When people see tangible improvements in their surroundings, they are more likely to participate, contribute, and advocate for continued change. This cycle of visible progress and increased involvement amplifies the impact far beyond the initial investment.

Resource Reallocation: A Balanced Approach

The question, then, is not whether to support international missions but how to balance our support to ensure our own communities also thrive. Consider the financial disparities: Billions of dollars are funneled into overseas missions annually, a testament to the generosity of individuals and organizations alike. Yet, imagine if even a fraction of these resources were redirected or equally matched by investments in intercity missions.

The argument isn't for an either/or scenario but for a more holistic approach to philanthropy and support. It's about broadening our scope of compassion and understanding that charity can, and should, begin at home without diminishing our global contributions.

A Blueprint for Change

So, how do we implement this vision of balanced support? It begins with awareness—recognizing the needs within our own communities and the power we must address them. From there, it's about mobilizing resources, fostering partnerships, and encouraging a culture of local volunteerism.

Governments, corporations, and individuals all have roles to play. Policies and initiatives that incentivize local support, corporate social responsibility programs focused on immediate communities, and platforms for individuals to contribute their time and resources to local causes are just the start.

A Call to Action

As we contemplate the future of support and philanthropy, let us remember that the strength of our global impact is rooted in the health and vitality of our local communities. By adopting a dual approach that values intercity missions just as highly as international ones, we pave the way for a more balanced, sustainable, and impactful model of support.

In western America and beyond, the potential for transformative change is immense—if only we choose to tap into it. Let this chapter serve not as a conclusion but as a beginning, a spark that ignites a broader conversation and a more equitable distribution of our collective efforts and resources.

Together, without guilt but with a deep sense of understanding and responsibility, we can foster change that resonates both locally and globally. In the vibrant yet challenged heart of southwest Florida, amidst the serene beauty and bustling communities, stands a beacon of hope and transformation—the City Takers Southwest Florida Mission Base. This formidable institution has emerged as a pivotal force in addressing the profound needs of the region, harnessing the boundless energy and commitment of its community to make a tangible difference in countless lives.

The Unending Stream of Hope

The City Takers Mission embodies the very essence of community support, serving as a testament to what can be achieved when compassion and action converge. With our doors open every single day, the mission welcomes an unlimited flow of individuals and families, each carrying their unique stories of struggle and hope. Here, the notion of supporting intercity missions becomes a tangible reality, showcasing the profound impact of local initiatives.

The Challenge of Scale

Despite the mission's Herculean efforts, the need within the southwest Florida area is vast, underscoring the imperative for a sustained and expanded response. The challenges are manifold, ranging from funding and resource allocation to volunteer engagement and program scalability. Yet, in the face of these hurdles, City Takers Mission continues to forge ahead, driven by a relentless commitment to its community.

A Call to Collaborative Action

To amplify its impact, City Takers Mission seeks the partnership of individuals, businesses, and other organizations within and beyond southwest Florida. This collaborative approach aims to pool resources, knowledge, and passion to address the multifaceted needs of the community more effectively. By fostering a network of support, the mission envisions a future where no individual or family in southwest Florida must face hardship alone.

Reflecting on the Journey Ahead

As we reflect on the transformative work of City Takers Mission Base, it becomes evident that supporting intercity missions can yield profound local and, by extension, global impact. The mission's journey is a clarion call to all who envision a world marked by compassion, resilience, and shared prosperity.

In southwest Florida and beyond, the path to meaningful change lies in recognizing the power of local action. By rallying around initiatives like City Takers Mission, we can collectively address the pressing challenges within our communities, forging a future where everyone has the opportunity to thrive. The mission's story is far from complete, but with each passing day, it writes a new chapter of hope, perseverance, and community empowerment. In the narrative of humanitarian efforts and philanthropy, the construction of orphanages abroad has long captured the collective imagination and goodwill of people worldwide. These endeavors reflect a profound commitment to aiding vulnerable children in distant lands, driven by a genuine desire to make a difference. However, amidst these commendable international efforts, a pressing issue lies closer to home, often overshadowed, and overlooked—the plight of orphans and vulnerable children within our own communities. This chapter seeks not to induce guilt but to broaden our understanding and to illuminate paths toward inclusive solutions that embrace the forgotten children in our own backyards.

The Overlooked Reality

Across the diverse and sprawling landscape of our nation, countless children find themselves navigating the complexities of life without the foundational support of a family. These children, much like their counterparts overseas, yearn for stability, love, and the opportunity to reach their full potential. Yet, despite the commonality of their needs, the plight of local orphans and vulnerable children often receives less attention and fewer resources than those far away.

The reasons for this disparity are multifaceted, ranging from the allure of aiding more 'exotic' locales to a simple lack of awareness about local needs. Moreover, the conceptualization of 'orphanhood' differs significantly across contexts, with many local vulnerable children living in foster care systems or in unstable home environments rather than traditional orphanages.

Shifting the Paradigm

Achieving a shift in focus requires a reevaluation of what it means to support vulnerable children. It calls for a recognition that the essence of such support—providing care, stability, and love—is universal and not confined by geography.

The following are key strategies to foster this inclusivity:

1. Raise Awareness: Illuminating the realities faced by local orphans and vulnerable children is the first step toward change. Through education and advocacy, we can shift the narrative to include the needs within our communities.

2. Engage Communities: Local support networks, including schools, churches, businesses, and civic organizations, play a

crucial role in supporting vulnerable children. By mobilizing these communities, we can create a robust support system that nurtures and empowers.

3. Expand Definitions of Support: Supporting vulnerable children in our communities can take many forms beyond the traditional orphanage model. Mentorship programs, foster care support, adoption awareness, and initiatives targeting at-risk youth can all make a significant impact.

4. Foster Collaboration: Partnerships between local and international child support organizations can foster knowledge exchange and amplify best practices. By learning from each other, we can enhance the efficacy of support for vulnerable children everywhere.

5. Empower Through Resources: Investment in local programs is crucial. This not only includes financial contributions but also volunteer time, skill-based support, and advocacy efforts. Such resources can transform the landscape of opportunity for these children.

A Collective Responsibility

INNERCITY MISSIONS

Addressing the needs of orphans and vulnerable children, both locally and internationally, is a collective responsibility that transcends borders and backgrounds. It reflects our shared humanity and the values that bind us as a community. By expanding our circle of compassion to include the forgotten children in our own backyards, we "the people" reaffirm our commitment to a world where every child is cherished and given the chance to thrive.

As we move forward, let us carry with us the understanding that our efforts to better the lives of children need not be an either/or proposition. There is ample room in our hearts and our actions for both the child far away and the child next-door. In embracing this inclusive approach, we can build a foundation of love and support that elevates all children, regardless of their circumstances or geography.

13 COMMUNITY

COMMUNITY THROUGH COMMUNICATION AND UNITY IN WESTERN AMERICAN CULTURE AND THE WORD OF GOD

In the heart of the Western American culture, where individualism often overshadows collective action, the essence of community has always been a beacon of hope, a testament to the power of coming together. The word *community* itself, a blend of 'comm-' from 'commune' and 'unity', serves as a profound reminder of what it fundamentally signifies: to communicate and unite, to become one tree from many seeds. This chapter delves into the significance of communication and unity in fostering a vibrant community, all while intertwining these concepts with the teachings of the Word of God, which has long championed the importance of fellowship and collective harmony.

The Roots of Community

To fully comprehend the essence of community, one must first understand its roots: communication and unity. To commune is to engage deeply, to share one's thoughts and feelings in a manner that bridges hearts. It's an act of vulnerability, of opening oneself to the influence and aid of others. Similarly, unity is about coming together, merging individual strengths to form a robust collective force. It's a testament to the idea that the whole is indeed greater than the sum of its parts. In a world that increasingly celebrates self-reliance, these concepts invite us to recognize the strength in numbers, the beauty in collective action.

Western American Culture & the Challenge of Unity

Western American culture, with its rich tapestry of diversity and individualism, presents both challenges and opportunities in the quest for community. The rugged individualism that defined the early pioneers has evolved into a societal ethos that often prioritizes personal achievement over communal welfare. However, within this challenge lies the opportunity for transformation. By embracing the principles of communication and unity, communities can transcend the barriers of individualism, fostering an environment where individuals not only thrive independently but also contribute to the well-being of the collective.

The Word of God & Community

The teachings of the Word of God deeply resonate with the concept of comm-unity. Scriptures are replete with passages that underscore the importance of fellowship, of caring for one another, and of working together towards a common goal. For instance, 1 Corinthians 12:12-14 metaphorically illustrates the community as a body, emphasizing that each member, despite their unique functions, is integral to the unity and functionality of the whole. This analogy beautifully mirrors the notion of community as a unified entity comprised of diverse individuals.

Furthermore, the Word of God calls for open communication, for speaking the truth in love (Ephesians 4:15) and bearing one another's burdens (Galatians 6:2). These teachings not only underscore the importance of transparent, compassionate dialogue but also highlight the role of empathy and support in strengthening the bonds of community.

Cultivating Community

To cultivate a healthy community within the context of Western American culture and the teachings of the Word of God, several foundational steps can be taken:

1. Foster Open Communication: Encourage environments where individuals feel free to express their thoughts, feelings, and needs without fear of judgment.

2. Promote Interdependence: Shift the focus from personal success to collective well-being, highlighting the importance of each individual contribution to the community.

3. Embrace Diversity: Acknowledge and respect the unique backgrounds, skills, and perspectives each person brings to the table, viewing them as strengths rather than divisions.

4. Engage in Collective Action: Unite in pursuit of common goals, whether they be for social, environmental, or spiritual betterment, demonstrating the tangible impact of comm-unity.

5. Align with Scriptural Principles: Incorporate teachings from the Word of God that advocate for unity, compassion, and mutual support, grounding the community in shared values and purpose.

INNERCITY MISSIONS

The journey towards a flourishing community in Western American culture, guided by the principles of the Word of God, is one of embracing comm-unity—where communication and unity serve as the roots from which the tree of community grows strong and resilient.

Made in the USA
Middletown, DE
16 July 2024

57381343R00097